THE SISTERS FROM CAMPOBASSO

DON DIMBERIO

———

WORN KEY
PUBLISHING

AVAILABLE IN EBOOK, PAPERBACK, AND HARDCOVER.

For my wife, who motivated me to tell this story.

To my mother and my aunts, because there is no story (nor my life) without their courage.

PART I
THE SON

CHAPTER 1

1 914.

"Don't shoot. I said I'm sorry, okay? I'll apologize. Please. Don't shoot."

Vico D'Imperio could hear his heart racing. He could feel it drumming in his chest. His hands were raised above his head, but they were shaking. Everything around him in the dark, empty street seemed to be a blur. The only object clearly visible was the shiny, silver revolver that glowed under a single streetlamp — its barrel pointed right at his chest.

It seemed like an entire year had gone by since he sat just a few hundred feet away, back inside Grotto Bar with his hand wrapped around a cold mug. But it had only been a few hours since the arms of other bar patrons were wrapped around him, restraining him after the fight. He could still smell the scent of stale beer that crawled into his jacket and left the bar with him. If he blinked, he could see the tables inside the bar thrown about and a gap that separated both sides of the bar — one side restraining Vico while the other attended to Mario. It looked as if the two men were entangled in vines, staring across the void at each other after a heated battle.

Had they never met, there may not have been a fight. Instead, Vico could have entered the bar that afternoon without concern. The trip to Grotto Bar could have simply been a casual visit, as it was to nearly everyone else enjoying themselves after a long day of work. Vico could have taken off his jacket, slung it over the back of a barstool, run his hands through his wavy, brown hair as he watched the barmaid pour his ale, and savored the atmosphere.

Instead, he walked in to find himself confronted with the face of a man that had done him wrong. A man that had abandoned Vico's daughters in a time of need even after being paid handsomely. That man was Mario Giuliani, the brother of a man Vico shared a rented room with. A short, pudgy man with a tiny nose and clean-shaven face that made those around him think he was actually worth the pennies that lined his jacket pocket.

Mario was laughing when Vico walked in. Joking around with those sharing a round table with him, half-full pitchers and mugs sitting before them. In an instant, Vico's mood had changed. He had gone from somber, missing his wife and wanting to drown his sorrows in a few mugs of ale, to enraged and frustrated all within a split second. It was like a switch had been flipped, and it ignited a fire within him.

His blood boiled as he walked across the wooden-planked floors, past an arrangement of tables — some empty, some full — and over to a vacant barstool. The ale he was served had a refreshing effect, but it didn't have the calming sensation he'd hoped for. Instead, all he could hear was Mario's voice as it carried across the bar. It took everything in him not to turn and hurl the mug across the room at the man. But he kept his cool. For a little while, at least.

It was only a few minutes later that Vico's right hand was covered in blood, and he was being pulled off of the man. Within all the yelling and screaming, Vico heard one chant roar through the crowd over and over:

"I'll kill you, Vico! You hear me? I'll kill you!"

Those words came from Mario's mouth as he stared down at the blood on his hands. It was seeping out of both nostrils and smeared across his cheek as he wiped with the back of his hand. No matter how hard he tried to clean up, he couldn't get himself

"Yes. Sorry for hitting you in front of everyone at the bar."

Vico just wanted to go home. He wanted to hug his girls and tell them how much he loved them. He wanted to write to his wife and tell her how excited he was—they were so close to completing the dream they sought out for their family over a decade ago. All they needed was her in America and a house to live in, and they would be set. They would be fully complete with their plan and their new life in America. The girls would have a better future, as would *their* children and *their* children after them. Vico could even envision how he would end this note to his wife, by telling her that she meant so much more to him than just the title of his wife. He would tell her how much he loved her and would end the note saying *See you soon* because he was confident that he would.

Mario's revolver was the only thing in his way. It was the only thing stopping him from hugging his girls and from writing that note to his wife. He opened his mouth to apologize to Mario once more. He didn't want to, but he didn't care anymore. The girls were all here safely with him so at the end of the day, it was a simple bad investment. Sure, Mario stole his money, but Vico had his girls with him now and that was the important part.

"Mario," he started. But it's all he would be able to say.

A loud bang echoed through the street, and it felt like Mario had taken a rock and threw it into Vico's chest with all his might. Only it hurt more than that. And it burned inside his chest. It was like a little ball of fire had torn through his skin and buried itself inside. Then another bang came followed by another, and suddenly there were three burning fireballs in his chest and Vico stumbled backwards. He tried to right himself, but the velocity of what hit him was too much to fight.

Vico knelt, clutching at his chest, desperately trying to pull out the burning balls inside him. But he couldn't. And suddenly he grew weaker. It was hard to breathe and when he coughed, liquid spattered out into his hand. He looked down, saw the dark red color, and felt his eyes widen.

He fell back into the street, and when his head hit the ground, it hurt him. But it was nothing compared to that horrible, burning feeling in his chest. Then he was looking up into the night sky. It was a clear night, and the stars were shining bright. As he looked up into them, suddenly the pain subsided. All he could focus on were the stars. He started naming them—one after his wife, Carmina, and then one after each of his three daughters: Loreto, Lena, and Carolina. They were the brightest four stars in the sky, and he was able to smile knowing he could find and name those brightest four. The brightest four stars in his life were now in the sky, where he knew he'd soon be.

Then the stars started to fade. All of them. The streetlamp beside him went dark, as did the stars, as did the night sky. And then there was nothing but black.

CHAPTER 2

 *resent Day.*

LOST. That was how he felt when he received word that Laura had died.

It had been two days since he'd gotten the alert. Two days since his cell phone buzzed on the table beside him as he enjoyed dinner in his quiet home in front of the TV.

The text message came from Abby, another of his cousins, and it read: *Mike, Laura passed away. I'm so sorry.*

The news certainly hurt Abby, too, as it did many other members of the D'Imperio family that had grown a few generations in America. Laura Ricci was a kind woman who had battled with a lingering heart condition and eventually lost. But for many years during her childhood and adolescence, she was more than just a cousin to Mike. They were children of sisters. Best friends. They did everything together, and the only reason they ever stopped was because adulthood had forced its way between the two. Although each had to move on with their life, they still remained in contact for many years, even after Mike would make the move to warmer weather in Arizona.

His flight was booked shortly after receiving the news. Within 36 hours he was out the door and on his way to the Phoenix Sky Harbor International Airport. The sky was dark when the Uber pulled into Mike's hardscaped driveway. The birds weren't chirping yet nor was there another light on in any other surrounding house. No dogs barked. No car engines turned. The only sound in the early morning was the humming of the air conditioners pushing cool air into the homes that would need relief from the midday heat.

Where Mike was headed, that wouldn't be necessary.

There wasn't another car on the road as his driver pulled through the streets of Paradise Valley. The world around him slept but that changed as they made their way closer to the airport that began to come alive. The baggage tugs and other little carts whipped around planes parked on the tarmac.

Mike was dropped off at the entrance to his terminal and thanked his driver. "Five stars, right?" the man asked in an accent that sounded almost Australian.

Mike had taken Ubers and Lyfts here and there but for the most part, his traveling days were over. He spent his years hustling his way into the business world, forming his own company. He knew the struggles of a business owner traveling to make sales and grow their organization, and many of those people made their way to the airport with him on that morning. But back when Mike was traveling for work, cabs were how someone got to and from the airport. And it was only five or six years ago that he'd slowed down, yet it felt like it had been decades with the way the world had been changing.

He gave his driver five stars, a smile, and a tip, and was on his way through the revolving doors to the security line. This process, too, was much different than when he first used to travel, but this was a change he was okay with. Better safe than sorry.

Pulling his carry-on behind him, he made his way through the terminal and to his gate where a few other passengers had already been waiting—some reading, some on their phone, and one sprawled out across a few chairs, sleeping. He confirmed the destination on the screen behind the gate's counter: Chicago. It was the pit stop he had to make before getting on a flight to his hometown of Cleveland.

The plane was at the gate, and the orange sky shone down onto the awakening airport. Mike took one long gaze out the window and into the scattered palms that sat in front of the brown mountain range in the distance. Caught in the window, in front of the view outside, was his own reflection. His gray hair. His glasses. All the signs of an aging man. The world seemed to pass by so quickly as he hustled his way into the successful businessman he was, but no amount of money made could bring back time. This was one reason he was able to so easily sell his business and fly off into the warmth of the Phoenix sun.

He ran his fingers through his thinning hair and then went to sit in one of the many empty seats. He debated between getting a coffee or pulling the neck pillow from his bag and decided on the latter—no reason to get the caffeine jitters for a three-hour flight. Especially not with a window seat. Instead, he pulled out his neck pillow and allowed himself to rest for a bit until it was time to board the plane.

Now boarding First-Class, priority card holders, and military members in uniform.

In his early days of flying, Mike would take the cheapest seat he could get. He could board Zone 20 for all he cared, as long as he got to where he needed to go to make his sale. Now though, retired and with some spare cash in the bank, he treated himself to a First-Class window seat.

I worked hard, he told himself. *I deserve it.* Besides,

going back home to say goodbye to such an important part of his life wasn't going to be easy. Cancer or not, expected death or unexpected, the loss of his cousin Laura still hurt.

He boarded, sat in his seat, declined the invite for a drink from the flight staff, and resituated himself in his seat with his neck pillow. Before he allowed himself to drift off into an early-morning nap, he reached into his wallet and pulled out a picture that had been there for so long. It was a family keepsake. Something to be cherished and never forgotten. It was a picture of his mother and her two sisters. The pride of their family. The strongest and most resilient women he'd ever come to know. For what they went through as children couldn't even be compared to what kids would call tough times today.

These three women were the glue of the family, and although they were gone they lived on in their children. Unfortunately, one of those children was to be put to rest. Mike was worried that with Laura's death came the reality that his generation of the D'Imperio family would all soon perish and his family tree would soon lose sight of his mother and her sisters. His fear was the D'Imperio family of the future wouldn't be able to appreciate all that they went through.

That was his fear, but he would try his best to educate the family on their doings. But first, he would allow himself to grieve for his lost cousin.

CHAPTER 3

$\mathcal{T}$he flight from Phoenix to Chicago was a long one, but the long distance from the cold is what made Mike choose Phoenix. After years of traveling in and out of airports in the north, battling the cold, the wind, and the snow, he was ready for a change. And he wasn't messing around when he made it—he moved to the desert.

Mike had been flying long enough to know the double-ding overhead meant the pilots were calling for their flight attendants. He watched ahead as the attendant closest to him reached for the phone connected to the wall and a smiling face nodded and mouthed something into its speaker before hanging up. A moment later, she was back on it and declaring the flight to be making its initial descent. *Please power down all large electronics and put smaller, hand-held devices in airplane mode.* It was a line he'd heard so

15

often in the days where his airline miles meant everything to him.

Now, though, his home in the warm desert with palms lining the street was what mattered. He would love to say it was his wife back home, or even his children, but he had neither. All he had in his life was a business, and it consumed him. The love of what he did drove him into the embracing arms of his company, but it also caused time to fly on by without making any stops. Marriage, kids, little league games, dance recitals. Mike's train had blown right by all those stops. He had no time to step off his train and soak in the memories that could have been made. He was focused. He had one goal, and it was to grow his business.

He built artificial intelligence, or AI, machinery. His products made the businesses he sold to perform better. Mike created industry-changing machinery. He was proud of what he and his organization were able to accomplish. And when he sold his company for what some would consider lottery winnings, he had no one to share it with. No wife or children. Not even a dog. He had employees and board members, but the relationships drifted as the months and years went on after the sale. They went on to become investors in other businesses, but Mike wanted no part of that. His train had hit its final destination. No ounce of him wanted to hop on another and start the entire process over again.

He had the sun, the pool, and the year-round warm weather and plenty of golf courses to keep him entertained. Part of him was sad he never had a family but then another part of him was okay with it. He never would have been home anyway. His kids would have barely seen him, and it's not like there was any video conferencing back then like there is today.

The only family he had was up north and on occasions like this, he would be happy to see them all, albeit the reason for his travels was a sad one.

But before he made it to Cleveland, he would have his layover in Chicago. After the flight attendant announced their descent and they made it through the turbulence that always comes with flying through clouds, he could see the land beneath, sectioned out to look like a map.

Whenever he had the privilege of flying into Chicago, he would hope air traffic control would take his plane to the east of Chicago O'Hare Airport, on the other side of Lake Michigan, where his alma mater sat. Mike spent four years at the University of Notre Dame before moving onto his career in business. While attending, many of his classmates were from prep schools and wealthy families, but he was just an Italian boy from Cleveland, a few hours east of the iconic South Bend.

Early on, it was tough for Mike to fit in with the rest of his classmates, but he was the first in his family to attend college, and he wasn't going to disappoint his family. After all, his mother and her sisters had been through so much worse. Their migration from Italy might have been one of the most gut-wrenching stories Mike had ever heard. It pained him to even think about his mother and her sisters going through what they did. The struggles. The fear. The heartbreak. It was like nothing he'd ever imagined. And it was all in the name of The American Dream that their parents—and many others at the time—were chasing.

The least he could do was power through his four years at the prestigious university and make a good career for himself.

And he did. He graduated with honors and then got into business where he was the president of two separate companies before forming his own. The little boy who grew up on Bellview Ave in the Asherville section of Cleveland had made a name for himself in the business world and defied the odds of what was expected of him. He was able to accomplish great things and truly found that American Dream his mother and her parents had chased. His mother and aunts lived long enough to see the roots of his success but were unfortunately not there to see the money he would make when selling his company. If they had, they would certainly be proud. Not only of Mike but of themselves—his grandparents for taking the risk to make the trip to America and his mom and her sisters for turning an awful situation into a positive one.

He hadn't known the extent of these stories as a kid roaming the streets of Asherville. The basics, yes. But the true, horrific details? He knew none of them. Nor did he know them when he was attaining his degree from the University of Notre Dame or running a successful business.

It wasn't until later in life that he would find out what truly happened. How one young girl's bravery was what led the entire family to be able to remain intact to this day.

CHAPTER 4

$\mathcal{W}$hen his flight touched down at Chicago O'Hare, he stepped off the plane to feel the rush of cold air that was trapped in the jetway. He thought about stopping right there and blocking foot traffic so that he could open his carry-on and pull out his jacket.

In fairness to the others, he decided against it. After all, this flight was coming from Phoenix and most of the passengers must have felt like they were thrown into a walk-in refrigerator after stepping off the plane. Surely, he wasn't the only one who had to go searching in the back corners of his closet for his *winter clothes* while packing for the trip.

Mike had a short layover in Chicago followed by an even shorter flight to Cleveland Hopkins International and another wave of cold as he stepped off the plane again. But he was finally there. Finally back home. Back to the place he was happy to escape after selling his company. Back to the place where he grew up and his family roots still held strong. And he was about to see them all.

He put on his jacket before he stepped onto the escalator that would bring him down below to the Rapid Transit. A chill filled the air as he descended and all he could think about were the lizards and iguanas that roamed free in his yard at home. There would be nothing here. Not this time of year. No insects, no reptiles, no anything. Just bundled up humans bustling their way to and from their destinations.

He made his way onto the train with the other bystanders as it approached and came to a halt. Mike took a seat in the car and waited until his stop on 125th Street before standing and exiting the car, and that's when he realized he hadn't felt cold yet. Not in the jetway, or in the underground Rapid Transit station. Those were chilly—this was *cold*. He zipped up his jacket, pulled his bag behind him, and started walking.

It had been ten years, but the directions to where he was going were still fresh in his mind. He would have felt the same had it been twenty years. The streets were a bit busier, and he didn't remember having pain in his knees—the *cold*—the last time he paced these streets. But other than that, nothing much had changed. As he walked the streets, he saw the stores he would visit as a child were all still standing. Carbone's Ice Cream Stand and Lornie's Bar and Grille had survived the test of time, still standing although the surrounding buildings and atmosphere had changed so greatly. Mike remembered some chatter, people walking, and a car or two driving by when he was a child walking down to the store with the money his mother gave him. Things were different now. Traffic. Car horns. Homeless people on the streets. It was much different.

Growing up, he noticed how the culture changed on the corner of 126th and Holland Avenue, where all these stores stood. As a teenager, Mike and the other guys his age would spend warm summer nights on the corner by Carbone's Ice Cream Stand in search of girls, though that would sometimes lead to fights. And then adulthood brought them to Lornie's Bar and Grille, where the number of fights seemed to only increase. Mike was never much of a fighter, but the girls were another thing.

Things were certainly different now.

Different, also, was the location of DiNucci's Grocery, which was standing proudly the last time Mike was there but not now. Now, it was a dollar store. And as Mike gazed into the window, he could see that the long countertops were taken out. They would hold cardboard boxes with all types of pasta and as a kid sent to the grocery by his mother with a few nickels in his hand, he could barely see past them.

"Go get some of those sewer pipes from DiNucci's for me, will you?" his mom would ask. *Sewer pipes.* It was what she called rigatoni. Mike chuckled at that many times as a teenager. "Get a loaf of American bread, too" she added. The Italian bread was delivered twice a week, American bread was bought in stores and used only sparingly. He could still taste the flavor and freshness of DiMarco's bread. He ate Italian bread all over the country as he traveled. None could match DiMarcos.

AND NOW IT WAS GONE. No more tall counter. No more boxes of pasta. No more sewer pipes to be sold to a young boy sent down to the store by his mother.

Times certainly had changed. But he wasn't too upset about it. Times were different now than they were when he was a kid, but that was a trend that had been carrying on for generations. Instead of dwelling, he simply allowed himself to remember the good times: playing ball in the street with other kids in the neighborhood, walking to and from school every day, being sent to the store by Mom, and growing closer to his cousin, Laura. They were close in age and therefore grew closest over the years. She was practically a sister to him.

And now there he was, only a few short blocks away from where he'd say his final goodbye to her before she would be laid to rest.

Times would change from generation to generation, and he was okay with that. But he wasn't ready for his generation to be pushed aside just yet. There was a story to tell, and he needed to get it out.

CHAPTER 5

*J*ust as he did as a young boy, Mike followed the beacon that was Saint Joseph's church. He made his way down Holland Avenue from 126th Street to 128th Street where the steeple of St. Joseph's Church still illuminated as it always had. Mike had been nostalgic to this point, but seeing this steeple was the icing on his cake. Seeing this made him feel like he was home.

St. Joseph's Church was just two blocks away from Bellview Ave, where Mike lived as a child. The street name was given to indicate the street's ability to see the bell atop the church, and it was a point of guidance for all who lived in the area of two-story rowhomes known as Asherville.

Despite the heavy population of Italian immigrants living in the area—Cleveland had so many Italians that it had a Big Italy and Little Italy section within the city—Asherville gained its name from a non-Italian. It was named after Richard Millsworth Asher, the son of the first family of shipping barons on the Great Lakes. Richard broke from his family's business and started his own foundry and ironworks, which ended up providing steady work to the many Italian men who came to the country seeking work, so they could save for their families to come as well. The wages were low, but the work was there, and many men coming over from the home country were grateful for the opportunity. The Asher Metalworks survived all the way up until 1960, lasting through two major world wars and the Korean War before folding. Offshore production and bad management were the ultimate demise of the company but not before it provided the opportunity for many Italian immigrants.

Italian name or not, Asherville had many immigrants from the old country, and it made for a feeling of comfort. And so too did the great beacon of St. Joseph's Church, born in 1921 by the same immigrants who came over from the old country. It was built and named in honor of the husband of the Mother of God, San Giuseppe. The Diocese had an Italian-American priest there for as long as Mike could remember. When Mike was a boy, many people in the neighborhood spoke no English, despite having been in America for several years. Having a priest who spoke the native tongue allowed many of the Asherville residents the ability to attend mass.

There were many memories of the place as a kid and one of those was counting each of the nine steps leading from the sidewalk to the entrance of the church. He did the same now, collapsing the handle of his carry-on bag he'd been wheeling around and lifting it by his side as he ascended and counted.

One...

Two...

Three...

He counted to nine and then reached for the door handle, just as he had done on so many occasions growing up. St. Joseph's Church was not only his place of worship but was also where he attended grade school.

Now, all these years later, he stood inside the entrance doors, looking around the quiet and empty church. He dipped his hand in the Holy Water, made a sign of the cross, and allowed himself to be in awe of the beauty around him. The tall ceiling, the altar made of marble, the statue of Saint Joseph and another of the Blessed Mother—the one that looked down on him for more than 60 years with her cloak of powder blue and the crown of jewels on her head. He thought of so many new churches that had put Our Lady away in a small corner. Mike had been inside this place so many times over the years and was enamored at its beauty. After all this time, it still looked vibrant. Even a non-religious person could admire it, Mike always thought.

He was anything *but*.

Mike's religious journey started with his mother. She set the stage for his Catholic upbringing by ensuring Mike never missed a Sunday Mass. His father, on the other hand, wasn't much of a church-goer. Not until the final year of his life when he was battling lung cancer was he able to find God and leave this world in a Holy state. A few short years later, a massive heart attack took the life of his mother. He knew undoubtedly that Ma had a high place in heaven, and he only hoped he could replicate her life so he too could find salvation.

He felt the same about Laura. His cousin. His friend. Whose funeral services would be held in this very church in less than twenty-four hours. In the same church where Dad's funeral took place. And Ma's. And many other family members and friends who grew up in Asherville. Decades ago, when they all showed up to this church every Sunday and walked the nine steps from the sidewalk to the front door, none of them thought about death. As children, when Mike and his siblings and friends would look up to their parents, no one thought about the time when they'd have to walk into this very church to say one last goodbye. No one thought about the years that would follow, where families who came to America from the old country would begin to split up. The world would become a busier place and travel would become more frequent. Some of the kids in the neighborhood would get job offers that would take them to other parts of the country. Some would stay. Some would end up in jail. And some would go on to form their own companies and retire in sunny Arizona.

Laura was one of the ones who never left. As kids, she and Mike were practically inseparable. But then adulthood kicked in. And responsibility. And Mike had to move on from Asherville, onto bigger and better things. Over the years, he always felt bad. He felt like Laura might have been stuck here but there was nothing either of them could do. She went on to have a family of her own and although Mike never felt as close to them as he did to her, he still remained in close contact.

The thought of the funeral instilled some fear into him. Throughout the years, he watched as his parents passed away and friends in the neighborhood close to their age. But Laura's passing seemed to be the start of a new generation on its way out. He knew that children of the family would be looking at him during Laura's mass, and they might be wondering when his turn would come. They would see an aging, gray-haired man and wonder, just as Mike had when he was young, what it would be like to be so close to the end. They would wonder about what he went through in life and what memories would be taken with him.

And for Mike, this was the scariest part about the death that would start to consume his generation of the family. He didn't want the memories to fade. He didn't want the stories to die out or be forgotten. His bloodline was still fresh in America, and his mother and her sisters fought like hell to survive in this place. They had to deal with the death of both of their parents. They were nearly separated, never to see each other again. They cried together. They struggled together. But most importantly, they stayed together.

Mike wanted to make sure that was never forgotten.

$\mathcal{I}$t had been years since he had seen Monsignor Cavillini but there he was, in the flesh, walking out from the back of Saint Joseph's church and standing behind the altar. His back slouched a little more than it had before, and the short, dark-haired man now seemed shorter and had balded and grayed. Mike still saw that compassion in him, though. As the Monsignor approached the altar boys who would help him to perform mass, he wore an empathetic grin on his face. It was one thing Mike remembered most.

Mike sat at the end of his pew towards the back of the church. Others dressed in black sat mostly in front of him, but he didn't want to join the ranks of close family just yet. He didn't want to disturb his cousin's service. He didn't want anyone to smile and hug him and gladly ask how he had been. Mike was ready to mourn Laura's loss, and it's what he wanted everyone else to do as well. He would save the catching up, hugs, and chit-chat for the luncheon that would follow.

The viewing took place in the early hours of the morning, and that's when most of the people let out their cries. Now, it was simply sniffles and awaiting mass to start. Looking up at the casket displayed by the altar, he thought about the number of deaths that had occurred over the years and the stories that died along with them. All the stories of family origin—of making their way from Italy to America in search for a new life. All of these stories were expected to be passed down from generation to generation, and Mike wondered just how many of them would. How many would be passed down and how many would be forgotten?

He reached into his wallet and pulled out the four Holy cards that he carried with him at all times. The first held a picture of his father, Joseph Dalberto. Beneath his smiling picture, the card read: *Born August 20, 1910; Died January 1, 1983.* The smiling face on the card was so important to Mike and how he went through his life. His dad was a great source of inspiration and guidance for him. Dad was the one who pounded the idea of college into his head ever since he was a little boy. He would go on and on about how great a college education could be and the benefits of having one. When he was older, Mike always asked himself, "How would he know? He stopped going to school after sixth grade."

Educated or not, his father had a lot of wisdom. He was a respected man in the community, a police officer all his life, loved and admired by both cops and crooks. Joseph Dalberto was an all-around good person and Mike felt like he carried a big part of his dad within him.

The other three Holy cards were the ones that reminded him of Laura's casket in the front of the church and how, as generations continued to go on in America, stories of origin would be lost.

The three cards were of his mother and her two sisters—The Three Musketeers of the family. They were the inseparable sisters whose journey through life was like a horror story and a fairy tale wrapped in one. It was the stuff novels are made of. The cards and dates in his hand read:

Carolina Dalberto: Born September 26, 1912; Died July 15, 1990

Lena Iorio: Born April 27, 1907; Died August 3, 1999

Laura Talamo: Born August 9, 1900; Died May 5, 1978

They were the family heroes. The ones who sacrificed so much to make this life in America possible for the family. Mike would never forget it. And while he was still alive, he was determined to learn more about their story and continue to pass it down to the new generations of his family. So determined, in fact, that he visited the old country six years prior to see what else he could learn.

The town of Mirabella, Italy was magnificent. It had cobblestone streets winding through neatly kept homes and buildings. It was an old city, dating back centuries, and there were no lawns as there would be in America. The homes lining the streets sat right on the sidewalk's edge.

The first stop he made while on his trip was to the cemetery of his grandmother who had passed away in 1916. She was an influential part of the story he'd heard so many times and never had the chance to visit the site where she was laid to rest.

As Mike approached the cemetery, he noticed a man sitting on a nearby bench and wondered who he was here to visit. Italy wasn't like America, in that it's been around for a much greater period of time. In America, cemeteries dating back to the 18th century are considered ancient while those wouldn't be considered as old here.

Mike went about his visit, leaving the man to mourn, or remember, or to simply visit the site of someone he loved. Whatever he was doing, he was doing so peacefully, and Mike planned to join him in doing so. He hadn't planned on having to bother the man, but when he noticed that there were no gravestones in the cemetery—only crypts—he had to ask *someone*, and the man was the only one around.

"Excuse me," Mike asked. "Where are the graves?"

It didn't hit Mike until he was done answering the question that he was in another country. English wasn't the preferred language here. Italian was. And Mike didn't know Italian well enough to speak it. Luckily, the man spoke enough English to understand and answer. He said that many of the old graves had deteriorated and the decision was made to use crypt burials only. All the remains of the deteriorated graves were gathered up and buried somewhere in a mass grave and the man didn't know where that was.

Although he wasn't able to see exactly where his grandmother was laid to rest, he was able to see a lot of the names on the crypts, and it was interesting to see the resemblance of so many names he knew in Cleveland. It reinstated what he had learned about the early 1900s when early emigrants who came to various places in America created enclaves of people of the same vicinity and background. They were known as paesani and were extremely close-knit to the point of establishing clubs and societies in America that reflected their historical cultural background in the old country.

After his attempt to visit his grandmother's resting place, he went to see the farm where she lived and raised her three daughters. The rugged countryside his oldest aunt spoke of so often was beautiful—she hadn't lied. And as he looked out into the green farmlands, he knew that this was where his grandmother, Carmina Fatica D'Imperio had worked so hard to make a better life for Mike's mother and her two sisters. His eyes filled with tears as he thought about the three girls, on this very piece of land, saying goodbye to their mother for the last time.

PART II
THE PARENTS

CHATER 7

1 *898.*

FISHING BOATS LINED the harbor in the Italian seaside town of Termoli. The town sat on the edge of Campobasso which ended on the teal waters of the Adriatic Sea. Grandma Carmina would never know it in her lifetime, but Termoli was blessed with some of the most beautiful beaches in the world.

Her youth consisted of being watched over closely by her parents, Gaetano and Angelina Fatica. Her father was a fisherman, as many men were in that town, and her mother was a homemaker. She would make extra money by baking goods and selling them to the townspeople. She was known around town for her cakes and pastries, and Carmina spent her youth learning the recipes.

There wasn't much she was able to do in her younger years. Both of her parents were strict with her, and her social life was nearly nonexistent. She would go outside and play with the other local kids from time to time, but most of her hours were spent with her mother, learning to cook, clean, sew, and do the household chores most wives were accustomed to doing in those times. And while that was taking place, her father was out on the water, catching fish and selling them to the local markets. He was able to provide a good life for his family, and in return all he asked was that his daughter and wife hold down their end of the bargain at home.

Carmina was a kid. She wanted to get out and explore. She had no idea how lucky she was to be living in one of the most beautiful places on Earth, but she wouldn't have known anyway. Still, despite her guarded life, Carmina was able to meet Antonio Patracca when she was a teenager. She wasn't allowed much leniency or time for fun, but when she was able to enjoy a bit of freedom, she tried to spend it with him.

Antonio was the most handsome boy she'd ever laid eyes on, and she knew she would marry him one day. He was tall, standing over six feet which, for Italians during that time, was towering. He was dark-skinned with jet black hair and had broad shoulders that she fell in love with.

This isn't to say that he was out of her league. She was a beautiful young woman herself, small in nature with olive skin and she was growing into her adult figure.

Carmina was fourteen when they first kissed, and Antonio was sixteen. The kiss came at dusk one clear and quiet evening as she walked the empty and peaceful streets of Termoli to deliver one of her mother's cakes to Mrs. Minadeo. Antonio jumped out and scared her so much she nearly dropped the cake.

"Antonio!"

He laughed. "Scusa! Scusa!" But apologizing didn't work. Antonio smiled, a big and enthusiastic smile as she hit his arm jokingly.

"Mi hai spaventato!" *You scared me!*

He apologized again and then walked with her on her delivery. They talked and laughed, and she had thoughts running through her mind of what life would be like for them when they got older. Antonio was a fisherman just like her father was, and she knew how to bake and care for a home just as her mother had taught her. They would be able to make a nice life together. They would have children and she would protect and care for her own children just as her mother and father had cared for and protected her.

The cake was delivered to Mrs. Minadeo, and then they were on their walk back to Carmina's house. Antonio wouldn't be able to walk with her for long, as Mom and Dad didn't know about Antonio and certainly wouldn't approve of her having a boyfriend. After all, they were even skeptical of her having *friends*—so a boyfriend was well out of the picture.

The sun was setting on the seaside, and as they walked together, talking and laughing, Antonio stopped her. *Come here*, he said in Italian: "Vieni qui."

She followed as he took her hand and led her into an alley between two closing shops. He spoke to her in his beautiful, deep voice. His dark eyes looking into hers as he held her hands. "Domani vado a pescare e tornerò tra due giorni." *I go fishing tomorrow and will be back in two days.*

Two days wasn't long. As the daughter of a fisherman, she knew all too well how these trips at sea worked. She would prefer he never leave her side, but she also knew that wasn't possible. She wanted to tell him to be safe. That she would miss him. That she would look forward to seeing him when he got back. But she wasn't able to because he grabbed her face and pulled her into his, kissing her and melting her heart at the same time. Carmina had never been kissed before. Never felt the warmth of another. Never felt the tingling sensation shoot down her neck and spine as her lips were locked on his. She knew right then, with certainty, that they would be together forever.

Then he pulled away, looked into her eyes and smiled. "Ciao," he said. And then he was off, running into the night. Expecting to see Carmina again in two days.

But that would be the last time either of them saw each other. The next day, one of the most horrific storms to ever hit Italy would crash into its east coast. The storm caused severe damage to the city of Termoli, but worse, caused devastation amongst the fishing fleet. The storm tore through the water, causing rough seas that wrecked ships and killed many fishermen.

Antonio was one of them.

Neither Antonio nor his father were ever heard from again. Their boat was never recovered nor were their bodies found. Twelve other fishermen who went out that day found the same unfortunate fate. Carmina was devastated at the loss of Antonio but at the same time grateful that her father had chosen not to go out to sea that day, for he too would have certainly been killed. He had chosen not to go out that day because his boat needed repairs. And that small, aging boat had remained in the family for two generations.

Carmina was grateful to have her father but

couldn't help but mourn for Antonio. Just one day before, they had kissed. He had looked deeply into her eyes, and they had a connection unlike anything she had ever been a part of. It was love. She knew it. And now it was gone. Just like that.

CHAPTER 8

The great storm of 1898 not only took Antonio, but it took many of the eligible young men of Termoli. That didn't matter to her parents, though. Gaetano Fatica believed his daughter would need a family in order for her life to have meaning, and he was determined to find her a husband.

In the small town of Termoli, Italy in 1898, losing a total of fourteen men in one day was catastrophic. Town populations then aren't nearly what they are now. This left a disproportionate ratio of eligible women to men to be married and start families. Carmina's father had alternative plans that involved searching for eligible husbands outside of Termoli.

Gaetano's brother, Bartolomao, had moved inland many years back. He grew tired of the sea. Fishing became daunting for him, and the idea of spending his life on a boat in order to survive wasn't something that interested him. So he took his chances elsewhere. He moved farther inland and started working for an uncle who owned land in the countryside. His uncle was kind enough to give him work —and even gave him his own small piece of land on which to farm—but Bartolomao still wasn't able to find success with it. He was never really driven the way Gaetano was. This was proven when their uncle grew tired of Bartolomao's laziness and sent him off elsewhere to work. He ended up finding work as a farmhand in Mirabella.

Being kicked off of his uncle's farm must have ignited a spark in Bartolomao because his work habits improved when he got to Mirabella—so much so that he became a favorite of local farmers and landowners when labor was needed. One of these foremen who favored the labor of Bartolomao was Domenico D'Imperio.

Domenico, along with his two sons, Lavico and Vincenzo, operated the farm they lived on. Years prior, Domenico's employer had given him a piece of land as a show of gratitude for many years of hard work. The small plot of land was on a hillside, looking up at the city of Mirabella. It wasn't the greatest piece of farmland—the soil was hard and the grounds rocky—but there was enough farmable ground to grow some crops. And where the land wasn't in good condition for planting, they had sheep.

Vincenzo wasn't pleased with the conditions, and he wasn't afraid to make it known. In Italian, he and Bartolomao had conversations as they worked beside each other. Vincenzo spoke of doing something more.

"I'm taking a trip to Termoli soon," Bartolomao told him. "I go every year to visit family. You should come with me. Take a break from this place."

"What do I want to go to Termoli for?"

"Something new? Try your hand at fishing maybe? There's a lot of potential to be on the water there."

"I want to farm," Vincenzo said, "just not under these conditions. We can't do anything on this land." He kicked the dirt when he said this and pieces of rock came up. He pointed. "See?"

Bartolomao couldn't blame him. There was much better land in Mirabella, and there was much more potential for growing more crops. He was upset that his dad hadn't found a way to get a better deal from the landowner who gave him this plot.

This was where he made mention of his niece, Carmina, who was in Termoli. "She pretty?" Vincenzo asked.

Bartolomao had often spoke of his family back on the east coast and mentions of his niece had caught the attention of some of the younger men. The conversation with the eighteen-year-old Vincenzo had the same effect.

"Alright. I'll go."

The date was set and the two men prepared for their journey. They would leave on March 17th, and the trip would take two days placing them in Termoli by the 19th, which was perfect timing. March 19th was the beloved feast of San Guiseppe. San Guiseppe was revered by the people of Molise as well as all of Italy. During the feast, Bartolomao and Vincenzo would be in Termoli, and they would enjoy eating panne fritta, the wonderful fried bread. It had been so long since Bartolomao had tried some, and he was excited to share it with his travel companion. Vincenzo, though, wasn't as worried about the bread as he was about meeting Bartolomao's niece.

Unfortunately, Vincenzo would have neither. The day before the two were set to embark on their trip, Vincenzo stumbled and fell while working. The result was a bruised and battered knee that left Vincenzo in no shape to walk around the farm, let alone embark on a long journey. Bartolomao was there to witness the fall, and all he could think about was his trip.

No festival.

No panne fritta.

What terrible timing, Bartolomao thought. *How could this have happened right now?*

It *was* terrible timing. The event was unfortunate,

but his desire to go for his annual visit to Termoli did not go unnoticed. That same day, while working on the farm, Domenico's younger son, Lavico, approached Bartolomao to let him know that he would go in his brother's place should Bartolomao wish. What he didn't know was that Lavico was forced onto this trip by his father who had empathized with Bartolomao.

But it didn't matter to him. He gladly accepted the new companionship along the journey, and the next day they were off on their trip that sent them 40 kilometers to the northeast.

CHAPTER 9

It was cold on the day they left the farm. There was a fine mist hanging in the air that covered the valley surrounding Mirabella. Lavico, or Vico as they called him, wasn't really in the mood for the trip, but he felt bad for Bartolomao. He was a good worker for Vico's father and a good friend of the family. Had it not been for Vincenzo's freak, untimely accident, Vico could have remained on the farm, working, where he preferred to be.

Instead, he was embarking on a journey that would take him across the country to Italy's eastern seaboard. Vico had heard of Termoli and the sea, but it was far enough away from his land in Mirabella that he never had the chance to see it.

The chill hung in the air as Vico and Bartolomao set out on their path, traveling across mountain ranges and vast areas of open land. On the way, they talked about many things, from work to the land they traveled and also about Bartolomao's niece, Carmina. To Vico, her uncle was very fond of her. He seemed to adore his family and loved his niece but felt the need to leave Termoli as it seemed any man who lived there would be confined to a life of fishing on the sea.

For Vico, all he knew was farming. His father had been a farmhand before he received his land, and then he continued to do so, teaching his sons the trade in the process. Vico knew that the land would be passed down to him and his brother one day and that would be their land to maintain.

The dampness of the day was taking a toll on the two, although they had made it nearly the entire length of the trip in one day. They were a mere 5 kilometers from Termoli when the sun went down, and they both needed some rest. They were able to find an abandoned shed where they could sleep. Vico found a place to lie his head and was completely unaware of how his life would change the next day.

Vico woke in the morning to the brightness of the sky shining in through planks on the shed. He wiped his face and then ran his hands through his wavy hair. Against the other wall of the shed was Bartolo-mao, still asleep. Vico stood quietly to avoid waking him, and then he stepped out into the daylight. Unlike the day before, the sun was out and there wasn't a cloud in the sky. There was nothing but green, grassy hillside surrounding their bunker from the night before, and Vico was ready to make the last leg of the journey.

He wasn't particularly excited about the trip when they left his father's farm the day before. But now, as they made their way closer to the shoreline, his disdain faded and excitement grew. He anticipated a fun time celebrating San Guiseppe and getting to see the waters of the Italian coastline—from where he stood, he could already *smell* the salt in the air.

By noon, Vico and Bartolomao were in Termoli. They wound their way down the cobblestone streets of the small town and stopped when they reached the door of Bartolomao's brother's house where a knock on the door would be followed by a great surprise for Vico.

Bartolomao talked about his niece and indicated to the men he worked with that she was a nice young woman. From what he said, she had learned the ways of homemaking from her mother and would be a good wife one day. What he failed to elaborate on was her true beauty. As she answered the door and threw her arms around her uncle in joy, Vico could do nothing but stare.

She was beautiful. Heavenly. Brown hair, brown eyes, olive skin, happy, radiant, and everything Vico could imagine in a perfect woman.

He listened as the two spoke. Bartolomao asked her where her dad was and she said he wasn't home

—he was mending nets down by the water. He asked his niece how she had been doing, and she asked him in return. And then Bartolomao turned and introduced Vico to his niece, Carmina, and he felt the spark.

She looked at him and said, "Ciao. Piacere di conoscerti." *Hi. Nice to meet you.*

All he could do was nod so that's what he did.

Had Bartolomao mentioned how truly beautiful his niece was, Vico might have been prepared for it. But he didn't.

The next few hours were spent getting to know Bartolomao's family and eventually meeting his brother, Gaetano. The entire city was preparing for the festival the following day that would celebrate San Guiseppe, and Vico helped in whatever way he could to prepare. Whenever he found a moment, he would talk to Carmina to see if she needed help but really, it was just to hear her speak. Everything about her was beautiful, even her voice.

At night, when Vico rested his head on a pillow under the same roof as Carmina, he could only wonder what this trip could bring for him. This trip that he was dreading just two days ago had now turned into something incredible. But he knew it wouldn't last forever. He would need to utilize the next few days of their trip making Carmina, Gaetano, and Bartolomao all confident that he could make a great husband and provider.

And that's exactly what he did. During the festival, he spoke with Carmina and with Gaetano and his wife, Angelina. He asked questions and sought answers he knew they could provide. He tried to make Carmina laugh and saw that he had succeeded on several tries.

His hard work would end up paying off, and his trip across Italy would prove to be one of the best decisions he ever made. Because eight months after Carmina and Vico met, they were married. On November 14, 1899, he married the beautiful young woman that he fell for as soon as he saw her.

CHAPTER 10

The move to Mirabella was tough on Carmina and Vico knew it, so he tried whatever he could to make sure she was happy. Her entire life had been spent by the sea and after their marriage, she had to leave to start in a place she had never known.

To try to prevent his new wife from becoming lonely and missing home where she was used to helping her mother, Vico told Carmina that he was ready to start a family immediately. And they did. Carmina was pregnant just a few short months after their wedding and nine months later, baby Loreto was born.

At the turn of the century, when Vico and Carmina had started their family and Vico was still working on his father's farm, things didn't seem so bad. They were making a decent life for themselves and they had food, land, and shelter. Carmina missed her life by the sea and the family would travel to Termoli when they could. But when Loreto was born, the traveling became more difficult. With a baby in the year 1900, any type of travel was difficult.

What they still had was their love for each other. Vico treated his wife well, unlike many husbands of his time. He never laid a hand on Carmina. Never expected that she walk on eggshells around him. He treated her fairly and in return, she loved him dearly.

But as the years went on, Vico started to become unhappy. Not with his family life but with his financial situation.

In 1903, Vico's father, Domenico D'Imperio, passed away. When he did, the land that he owned was split between his two sons, Vico and Vincenzo. But Vincenzo wanted nothing to do with the land. He had been disgruntled about working on the harsh and rocky soil since their dad acquired the land from a nearby farmer. So when Domenico passed away and the land was distributed, Vincenzo had given his portion to his brother.

But Vico still struggled. He couldn't tell if it was the land that was the problem or the fact that he wanted a better life. While his dad was operating the land and he was a young boy growing up, he never had an issue with it. But now, as a father and a husband, he felt like he wanted more. He had pulled Carmina from her little town and brought her back here and for that he started to feel bad. He felt like he had pulled her from what she knew in order to sit at home and tend to a house and a baby. He wanted better for her. And he wanted better for baby Loreto.

Soon after his father's death, he approached Carmina to discuss what he was planning: He intended to move his family to the United States.

At the time, Italy was going through some intense conflicts. The north and south were butting heads. The entire country was going through a suffrage movement, and the south was getting the worst of it. Government was helping the northerners but was openly criticized for not helping the poor people of the south. These tough times had caused many Italians to flee the country and take a chance at life in the United States.

Vico wanted to be one of them. He didn't want his wife or his daughter to be looked down upon by the arrogant people of the north. Carmina would tell him stories of how the northerners would come to the pristine beaches of Termoli for vacation and would consistently belittle the locals. They were snobbish and rude and Carmina, when a young girl and a teenager, would often cry at some of the hateful things they would say.

Vico wanted a better life for his family. A life of wealth and freedom. A life the American Dream could provide. A life away from the consistent back-and-forth bickering going on in their home country.

He approached Carmina and let her know of his intent. His uncle had left Italy four years prior and was making a good life for himself in America, and Vico wanted to try it for himself. But the move couldn't be sudden. He didn't have the money to simply pack up and go. So he and Carmina agreed on a plan: Vico would go to America for one year to try it out and see if they could truly make a life for themselves there. This was an extremely common practice of the time, and many Italian men were doing so. They would explore America and see if there really *was* opportunity enough to move their family there. And once they would find work and save enough money, they would buy prepaid tickets for their family and mail them home. The prepaid tickets were almost always for steerage passengers, but the families would make the sacrifice for the promise of the new land.

Vico knew the move was going to be tough. It would be for both him and for Carmina, who would now be left alone with Loreto who was now three years old. But the risk could have a big reward, and Vico thought the tough times would be worth it in the end. So many Italians were making the same move during this time and reports of good things were making their way back to the old country.

His uncle and his family had made the move to America in 1900. It was his mother's brother who went and they had found a home in the city of Cleveland, which is where many Italians were finding themselves a home. And for many Italians, money was an issue. Both northern Italy and southern Italy had populations of poor although the government decisions were causing many of the southerners to embark on the trip across the Atlantic. This meant a lot of poor Italian immigrants were making their way to the United States and would have nowhere to stay. They couldn't afford to buy a home. Boarding houses were a popular type of living arrangement for this reason. The men of Italy would come to America to find work and would send money home to their families. Some would work for a few years and then go home while others tried to save enough money to bring their families to the U.S. permanently.

The plan was for Vico to work for a year and then he and Carmina would determine what was the best situation for their family. As the days went by and Vico came closer to leaving, the excitement and anticipation grew, but so did his feelings of nervousness and sadness. He was about to go on a journey where he wouldn't see his wife or daughter for a year or more. It was going to be tough. He was going to be lonely, and he knew the loneliness would creep up on Carmina, too. Luckily she had Loreto.

The final night before he was set to leave, Vico laid in bed next to his wife and they held each other close. His bag was packed and by the front door. All arrangements had been set up to travel. All he had to do was get himself to the Naples dockyard the next day where his ship would be waiting.

His head was on the bed beside his wife's, and he grabbed her cheek and rubbed it with his thumb. "Andrà tutto bene," he told her. And he meant it. Everything *would* be alright. He would make sure of it. It was going to be a difficult first few days or weeks to get adjusted, but it would all work out. In the end, they would all be in America and happy.

He barely slept a wink that night and instead stared at his wife. Occasionally, he would get up and walk over to the bed that held his three-year-old girl and couldn't help but let tears flow down his cheeks. He knew the next time he saw her, she would be different. Bigger. He would never again see her as she was at that very moment.

When the sun rose and it was time for him to leave, Vico kissed his sleeping daughter and then walked to the door with Carmina. They held each other close and Vico couldn't contain the lump in his throat. He and his wife cried at the thought of being apart for so long. They promised to write each other as much as they could. Vico would tell her where he was and how things were going, and Carmina would tell him about Loreto and how she was growing.

Vico wanted to hold his wife forever. He didn't want to let go of her. Didn't want to say goodbye. But he knew he had to leave. If he didn't, he would regret it forever. Their family would remain struggling on this farm, being criticized by northerners and by their government, and they may never have another opportunity to go.

With a broken heart, Vico pulled away from his wife. He leaned down and picked up his bag, tossed it over his shoulder, and then he walked out of the house. As he made his way down the road, he listened for the sound of the door to their house closing, but it didn't come. He could feel his wife's watering eyes on him with every step he took. But he didn't want to turn around. He didn't want to contemplate staying again. He couldn't. This was the best move for his family's future, and he knew it.

As much as he told himself not to, he gave in to the temptation. He turned around and saw what he knew he would see. Carmina was standing in the doorway. And she was crying.

CHAPTER 11

$\mathcal{A}$fter Vico left his home, his crying wife and his sleeping baby daughter, he was all alone. The morning mist held low over the grassy hills of the Italian countryside as he made his way 23 miles from his home to the Naples shipyard. The walk was long, but he was used to the long walks across the terrain as a lifelong farmer. And this journey would all be worth it in the end because his family would one day have a nice life in America.

Hiking through the vast hills and paths, Vico wasn't alone. As he made his way closer on the journey to the shipyard, he would find the presence of more and more fellow countrymen making the journey as well. Some came to the shipyard by wagon, some by donkey, and still others by foot.

The trip was long, but it certainly wasn't lonely. Record books would show that in the year Vico left for America, in 1903, over 200,000 Italians emigrated from the divided country and into America. So while his family wasn't with him, there were plenty of other countrymen on the same quest. Still, others had already made enough for their families to make the trip, and those families had made their way to Naples as well.

The SS Ancona was the vessel that would take him across the Atlantic. It was a large ship for the time. A passenger vessel that held first- and second-class passengers in its upper decks, and the steerage passengers down below. At exactly midnight on August 23, 1904, the ship set sail from its port in Naples, Italy, and headed to Ellis Island off the coast of New York.

Vico found himself in steerage with many other poor citizens of Southern Italy. Their lower-deck rooms had no view of the ocean, and when they were able to manage their way to a designated outside deck for steerage passengers, they found themselves getting covered with dirt from the stacks of the ship that rose up and out like long pipes into the sky.

But it wasn't the view of the ocean that Vico was worried about. He wasn't concerned about the fresh air. He sat along the benches lining the halls of the lower steerage deck, eating the meals provided during the journey, and writing letters to Carmina that he would send once in America. He hated the idea that his wife and daughter would have to one day endure the journey. It was a rocky fourteen days at sea, with heavy winds and strong ocean waves sending the ship rocking back and forth. Many of the steerage passengers had never been on a ship, and the rockiness caused a great deal of them to become sick onboard.

It would all be worth it, though. That's what he told himself. That's what so many of the sick and lonely passengers on the ship told themselves.

It was all going to be worth it.

And then, the time finally came. It was the moment he'd thought about for so long. He traveled many miles by land through Southern Italy to get to the shorelines of Naples and the SS Ancona that would transport him across the Atlantic. After all the heartache and the headache, he was finally able to see what he had only imagined would one day be before him. On the only day Vico D'Imperio cared to maneuver his way onto the steerage viewing deck, he looked out into the ocean ahead and was looking at what he knew was the Statue of Liberty. It was a sight his uncle—the one who had come to America three years before—and many other Italian families had spoken about. It was the symbol of a new life. And while Vico didn't have his wife and young daughter there to celebrate with him now, he knew the steps he was taking would one day lead to them coming to the new country.

He hung over the rails of the wooden deck of the

SS Ancona to look out into the dark blue waters of the Atlantic Ocean. The ship traveled through the ocean's waters and made its way slowly into the New York Harbor where the patrons of the ship would soon depart. In only a short period of time, Vico would step foot on American soil—something so many back home in Italy spoke of but would never experience. And yet here he was, watching as Ellis Island grew ever-closer to the bow of the ship.

The ship stopped for a lengthy period of time and Vico knew why: officials from the U.S. had done their customary entrance aboard ship to ensure no major diseases or outbreaks had spread. Before the ship could come to Ellis Island, they had to be sure everyone was safe. The officials did this for the first- and second-class passengers, while steerage passengers were summoned to Ellis Island. And this was fine with Vico. He had traveled so far to get to this point. He could wait a few more hours

And when a few hours passed and officials had departed the ship, its engines roared once more and the SS Ancona was headed north toward the skyline of New York City. Vico knew he would soon step foot onto U.S. soil. But first, the ship went slowly by the Statue of Liberty.

A mixture of sobs and cheers surrounded him as he stared intently into the statue's features—its towering structure, the lit torch at its peak—he heard the excitement grow around him. For so many others on this vessel, this was their sign of freedom. Many others on this ship made incredible sacrifices to be able to witness this moment. They'd left behind their entire lives to come find hope in a new place. They had left behind family members, jobs, and everything they knew.

Vico could feel the emotions of the others in this situation because he had also sacrificed so much to come here. The site of his arrival to the United States was bittersweet. He was finally in *The Land of Opportunity* but all alone.

The SS Ancona made its way to port at Ellis Island, and the level of excitement in the passengers around him was growing. Adults were dancing, children were waving small flags of their new country, and the ship was inching closer and closer to its final resting spot where it would pour off all the happy souls into their new life.

Unfortunately, not all who danced and celebrated would make it through to the other side of the New York Harbor and into America. Some would be turned away for medical reasons, such as health issues or mental instability. Pushing the small chance of rejection from his mind, Vico allowed himself to be optimistic about what this country could bring. The Statue of Liberty was a sign of freedom from the political turmoil occurring in Italy.

Once the SS Ancona docked at Ellis Island, Vico threw his bag over his shoulder and headed with the steerage crowd toward the exit. He had no idea what would happen, or where he would go from here. He only knew what he was being told.

American workers were shouting. He had no idea what they were saying. But on his way out, he had a sticker slapped onto his chest by a man in a police hat, and the number read *46*. He looked at others around him and saw a variety of numbers. Vico was confused. Everything was so fast-paced. He wasn't back on his farm. He was in a new country, where no one seemed to speak Italian. Where was he supposed to go? What was he to do? He needed to find the train.

"Treno?" he asked with his palms in the air. "Treno?"

"This way!" another man with a police hat shouted and pointed him towards a group standing together.

He followed and when he got there, he noticed others wearing the number 46 on their clothes. Close to 20 or 30 of them. All looking around. All confused.

"Chi parla italiano?" a man standing in the middle of the crowd asked.

"Lo voglio! Lo voglio!" Vico said. *I do! I do!* But his voice was drowned out by the others in the group. There were so many. He felt comforted knowing this.

"Per di qua!" the man shouted and waved his hand for the crowd of 46's to follow.

Vico followed the flow of passengers into what he

would later find out was called Great Hall, where physical and mental examinations would take place. It was a towering building, filled with hope and promise and would eventually see 15 million immigrants pass through its halls. The 46's were all brought up the marble staircase and set into lines. Vico was directed to a line of men—women and children brought to a separate line—where he would be examined by doctors. He didn't know it at the time, but doctors were standing by, observing, looking for signs of sickness in the passengers that made their way up the staircase.

Vico was used to long and agonizing walks. Used to spending time on his feet. He was neither sick nor out of shape, and the stairs had no impact on him. He made his way to the top and into his designated line where he would await his physical evaluation in what was called the Registry Room.

The line inched along and as he got closer to the front, he could see the holding cells where the *ill* or *unable to process* were being held. He watched as some of the people were being escorted from the front of the line with white marks drawn on their foreheads. There were cries and pleas but no budging from the U.S. officials. Vico could think of no worse fate after all the trouble he'd gone through than to be rejected from entry to this new and optimistic country.

As the line moved and he approached his turn to

be examined, he could feel himself shaking. Was this really it? Really happening?

Vico made it to the front of the line and found himself face-to-face with a doctor that had the determining say in whether or not he could enter the country. The doctor approached him and spoke some words in English—a language Vico didn't know. The doctor continued to speak, and Vico noticed he was speaking to his associate. The doctor signaled for Vico to remove his shirt and then examined his chest, his stomach, his head, ears and mouth. With each new motion of the doctor, Vico became more tense.

There's so much riding on me getting in. I need this. My family needs this.

And then a set of words came from the doctor that Vico once again couldn't understand. But what he *did* understand was the head-nod, gesturing for Vico to move along.

He grabbed the bag he had held by his side since the day he left the Italian countryside and he flung it over his shoulder. He nodded in appreciation and then hurried along.

Next, he went into what was called a *primary line* where he was asked a series of questions—31 of them to be exact—through an interpreter. The questions ranged from *Why are you here?* to *Do you have a criminal past?* to *What are your intentions?* and were meant to filter out those who may be there for the wrong reasons. Vico had none. He was simply there to give his family an opportunity at a better life.

After passing the primary line, Vico was given the nod of approval to enter the country. It was a proud moment for him. One of joy and promise and hope. He followed the others as they made their way through the Great Hall doors and back outside where they made their way to the other side of the island famously named The Kissing Post, where families already living in the United States would meet to welcome their relatives. While Vico had no one at the Kissing Post waiting for him, he *did* have family in Cleveland, where many Italian immigrants were beginning to migrate to at the time. There, he would meet with his Uncle Francisco Mastrangelo, his mother's brother who everyone called Uncle Charlie and who had been in the U.S. since 1900.

Vico walked through the crowd of happy and smiling families and entered the ferry that would take him across the harbor and into New York City, where he could then begin his journey west. He was getting closer to his new life, yet continually placing more distance between himself and his old one—something he would one day regret.

CHAPTER 12

*V*ico was in. He had passed his tests, and the final thing he needed to do while on Ellis Island was to arrive at the Money Exchange to purchase his train ticket and exchange his Italian currency, lira, for dollars. And once he did, he was on a ferry and moving across the harbor, away from Ellis Island and closer to The Land of Opportunity.

Stepping off the ferry, Vico's first immediate thought was that New York City was much busier and thriving more than anything he knew back home in Southern Italy. There seemed to be hundreds or even thousands of people moving about, everywhere he looked. There were buildings along the streets made of brick and several stories high—taller than anything he'd seen built back on the grassy hills of Mirabella. The city was certainly developed, and Vico was struck with astonishment.

The interpreter that helped Vico from the SS Ancona, through Great Hall, and into New York City had also helped point him in the direction of the train station. And then that was it. Vico was on his own. In America. Needing to go nearly 500 miles west to Cleveland where Uncle Charlie would be there to meet him.

The conditions on the train weren't nearly as harsh as the SS Ancona—and the trip wasn't nearly as long—but the train wasn't as comfortable for newly-arriving immigrants as it was for Americans. Immigrants were placed into train cars made of tile and wood while those designed for American citizens were comfortable with soft seats and varying amenities.

Again, Vico wasn't concerned about being pampered. Compared to where he came from, a train ride in its own was something new and adventurous to him. And he would soon find that the conditions where he would eventually work were much worse.

When the train arrived in Cleveland, Ohio, Uncle Charlie and his wife, Aunt Tomasina, were there to meet him. It was a long and grueling trip—the long walk to the Italian coastline, the two weeks aboard the SS Ancona, the 500-mile train ride to Cleveland—but Vico was finally there. Finally in his home in America. Finally where he would be able to start working and creating what would hopefully be a life for his family.

Cleveland wasn't nearly as populated as New York City, but it still had a lot of people compared to what he was used to back home. Vico walked the streets with his aunt and uncle and went back to their house where they spoke, and Aunt Tomasina made dinner—something she would do for him almost every night. Uncle Charlie let Vico know that he was able to get him a job at Asher Metalworks and found him boarding at a local boarding house run by a nice woman named Mrs. Carlluci. Vico, ever-grateful, threw his arms around his aunt and uncle before parting ways that night and making his way to his new living quarters.

Mrs. Carlluci was a nice woman and, as Vico would find about so many people in Cleveland, she spoke Italian.

Boarding houses were common amongst the men who came to the country to pave the way for their families to follow. The rooms were shared, but it was enough for them all. The only things they needed were a bed and a shelter from the cold winter months in Cleveland. Vico was perfectly fine with making the sacrifice if it meant he could see his family come to America soon.

On his first night there, he wrote a letter to his wife. In the morning, he would send her every letter he wrote during the trip, along with the one he wrote that night. This would let her know all about his voyage and that he was safe in Cleveland with work and a place to lie his head at night.

> *August 1904*
> *Dear Carmina,*
> *I have arrived in America and settled in*
> *Cleveland. Uncle Francisco has helped*
> *me so much. America is so exciting.*
> *When our ship entered the harbor and I*
> *saw the Statue of Liberty I wished so*
> *that you and Loreto could have been*
> *with me. I will start my job at the*
> *foundry this week and I look forward to*
> *earning money so we can all come to*
> *America. You will like Cleveland as*
> *there are many paesani here and many*
> *customs from Campobasso are followed.*
> *Please take care of yourself and my*
> *beautiful Loreto. I have included the*
> *letters I wrote while on the boat. They*
> *helped me make the journey faster.*
> *Love, Vico*

Mrs. Carlluci's house was the largest house on 126th street. It had seven bedrooms, four of which were shared and the other three were offered at a premium price of $3 per week. But most of the men who stayed at the house were there for one reason: to save and bring their families over. Most of the men were from the same parts of Southern Italy where Vico came from and staying in Mrs. Carlluci's house felt almost like home at some points. Vico befriended most of the men and each had either a wife back home or a girl they had planned to marry.

October 1904
Dear Vico,
I was thrilled to receive your first letter
    from America. I enjoyed so much the
    letters from the voyage. Things are fine
    here but I miss you very much. Loreto is
    so beautiful and so much help to me.
    The Fall has been very warm and I had
    no trouble harvesting our crop. Also I
    have sold two sheep. Our flock is down
    to eight but very healthy. I long to be
    with you in America and know someday
    it will happen. Please be careful with the
    women in America. Mila Santucci's
    husband Nello has written her that he
    has met an American woman and will
    not return. She is crushed. Her brother
    has sworn revenge when he gets to
    America. Be careful!
Love, Carmina

Most men were young, in their very early 20s or younger. And the temptation of being alone in America had gotten the best of them. They became involved with women in America and abandoned their wife or girlfriend in Italy. The women in the home country were left to fend for themselves. No more husband or husband-to-be. But the risk these men took in doing this was high. Their lives were put in great danger. The paesani, another name for the other Italians in Cleveland, would beat them badly, sometimes even killing them. Since there were so many people in Cleveland who came from the same Italian towns, word would spread around pretty quickly. And the end result wasn't good for the men who abandoned their women back in the home country.

Vico didn't get wrapped up in the other women in America. He would occasionally join the men of his boarding house for a beer or two after a long day of work, but that was all. He had one goal by being in America, and he knew the most important thing he could do was save his money. So he worked and he saved. His job at Asher Metalworks was as a foundry helper, and it was grueling. The conditions were hot and dirty, and the job consisted of handling the sand molds after the hot metal had been poured into them and cooled. It was tedious and dangerous, but that turned out to be a benefit for Vico because no one else wanted to do the job. It allowed him to have job security and after one year of work, he was able to send $200 home to Carmina to help out.

> *September 1905*
> *Dear Carmina,*
> *I am sending you this two hundred dollars I*
> *have saved since coming to America.*
> *Use it where it is most needed. I am*
> *beginning to plan to come home in the*
> *next eight to ten months. I can't go too*
> *much longer without seeing you and*
> *Loreto. Work at the foundry continues*
> *to be hard and dangerous. I don't mind*
> *as I know what it will bring.*
> *Love, Vico*

Vico watched as people left the boarding house and new people came. Some of the men went back home, and some stayed as their families were making their way over and they would move out of the boarding house and into a home of their own. This was the future Vico envisioned, and it was what drove him to keep his head down and work hard. He didn't allow himself to get sidetracked by the women or other activities some of the men fell for.

In July of 1906, his time finally came. After two

years of working in America, he was ready to travel back home to Carmina. Once home, the two of them would begin their plan to come to America.

Only this time, they would come together.

July 1906
Dear Carmina,
The time has finally come. I will be coming
home in mid-August. I have booked my
passage and will depart New York on
July 19th. My arrival time in
Campobasso will depend on the ship's
time for the voyage and my getting from
Naples to Mirabella. My heart is so
excited to see you, Loreto and my town.
I will see you soon my love.
Love, Vico

CHAPTER 13

*C*armina could remember the morning Vico left her like it was just the other day. It had been two years since she saw her husband's face, but she could still feel his warmth in their bed. She had his letters beside her pillow, and she would read them each night before she went off to sleep. She felt comfort in knowing that with each passing night, she was one day closer to seeing her beloved Vico again. But still, two years was a long time. And he left her a lot to care for in his absence.

It was in August of 1904 that he departed, walking away with his bag over his shoulder and leaving her in the doorway, crying, heart wrenching and wishing that there hadn't been such a horrible situation occurring in their home country of Italy. Had the north and south not been at each other's throats, Vico wouldn't have been driven to the idea of traveling to America.

But it had. The turmoil in Italy made Vico want to travel and now, two years later, he was on his way back.

During those two years that he was gone, she did everything. She worked hard to maintain her small plot of land left by Vico's father when he passed. There were ten sheep on the land that she also cared for. Carmina was proud of herself for the job she'd done on the farm as well as raising Loreto, who was now a marvelous little girl almost six years old. To Loreto, the sight of her father might be more shocking than it would be for Carmina. Although they spoke of him every day, it was his sight that Loreto hadn't seen for nearly one-third of her life.

Her last correspondence with her husband was through a letter that stated he was expected to return to Naples on August 10th. Each morning after that, she looked out for him. It would take him a few days to make his way across the countryside and she had to be patient, but it had been so long since she was in the loving arms of her husband. She was excited to feel his warmth. His arms. And to feel his lips on hers.

She waited for him by the door and looked for him to appear while attending to the farm. She looked up to the top of the hill where Vico would soon walk over and then down into the valley where he would be home again. Day became night and then another day and night came. The anticipation was almost too much for Carmina to handle, but it was much better than the emotional struggle she had gone through for the previous two years.

On August 12th, as Carmina put Loreto to bed, she heard footsteps come across the stone path outside. She rushed to the door to find it was only Tomas Ranallo returning from his daily trip from Oratino. Tomas was a nice man, and his daily trip carried him through the farmland of Carmina. She would stop to have a conversation with him on occasion. Considering she lived in a secluded area and didn't have many people to communicate with, his presence was almost always welcomed. But on some instances, she could feel his desire for more. Carmina was young. And she was pretty. More importantly, she was lonely. And although she wouldn't think of hurting her husband, the thought of another's touch warmed her. To be in someone's arms again would be nice. Tomas was one of the only people she saw, and she could tell from his occasional actions that he would be receptive to the idea.

On this night, she simply waved to him and he waved back, continuing on his path home. Once Loreto was asleep, Carmina put her head on her pillow and reread some of Vico's letters from when he first made the journey to America. She read what he wrote about the vigorous seas, the steerage accommodations, and the first sight of the Statue of Liberty. Carmina hoped his travel home across the Atlantic wasn't as harsh as the first one, but knew he wouldn't be worried about seasickness if it meant coming home to his wife and daughter. After a while, her eyes finally grew heavy. She extinguished the lamp beside her and closed her eyes, hopeful that she would be awoken by her husband's touch.

Another day came and went with no sign of Vico, and on the morning of August 14th, Carmina cried. For days, she had wondered where Vico could be. Over the years, she had heard the horror stories of local men from Campobasso and Mirabella going to America and never returning home. Instead, they met and fell in love with American women. Carmina had always had the fear of Vico falling in love with an American woman in the back of her mind, but she never thought it could be true. She assumed it was simply paranoia. But when Vico hadn't returned four days after his ship was scheduled in Naples, the idea of him not coming back had hit her like a wave. She was lost again. Alone. She had lost Antonio before and now had lost Vico. She found herself alone again.

Carmina pictured Vico writing that final letter to inform her that he was heading to the vessel that would take him home, only to mail the letter and turn to his new love, leaving Carmina in Italy to fend for herself.

The thought hurt. With each passing hour, it was

like the visualizations were becoming more real. There was still hope that he would come walking over the hill, but it was dwindling. On August 14th, as she worked out on the farm, she found herself looking up at the hilltop less and less. She couldn't take the disappointment anymore. As the sun began to set and she started cleaning for the day, her heart hurt. She was nauseous. Two years she had waited for him. And after all that time, she was finding out there would be no more *him*.

Before she went into the house for the night, she turned one last time to look up at the hilltop. She knew there would be nothing there, but she wanted to envision it anyway. It was an image she had wanted to see for two years, and although she now had to admit to herself that it would never happen, she still wanted to imagine it. As she looked up to the hilltop, she allowed herself to see it. To see *him*. Vico. Walking over the top of the hill and making his way down to the slope towards the farm. The vision she wanted to see was of him walking slowly down the hill, a man who had been tired from his travels and needed to slowly make his way into his home. But her eyes wouldn't let her see that. Instead, they showed her an image of Vico running, his bag dropped to the ground as soon as his eyes met hers and a giant grin across his face.

In this vision, he looked older. Worn. More of a man. But he was a happy man. And as the figure of his body got closer, she turned to the house. She allowed herself to say goodbye to him this way. That would be the last time she would see his face. The last time she would see her husband. She and Loreto would get along in life without him from now on. She was ready to accept that.

But then a hand rested on her shoulder and spun her around. Vico was now standing right before her eyes, and she reached out to touch his face. It was him. Vico. In the flesh. Not a mirage. Not an image. He was really there. Smiling. He grabbed her face and pulled her into his, and his lips were real. They were warm. Dry, but warm. And he held her face against his for what seemed like a full minute before he let her go and before she could even gasp, her body reacted the way she wanted it to for the two years she pictured this very day:

"Loreto!" she yelled. "È papa!" *It's Daddy!*

CHAPTER 14

The smell inside Asher Metalworks was one of smoke, fire, and sweat. The air was hard to breathe inside the building, but Vico had no choice but to inhale. On some occasions, back in the room where he stayed at Mrs. Carlluci's house, he would get a whiff of what smelled like Carmina. It was a world of difference from the fumes he had to take in during his workday, and it was an escape from where he was. It was as if for one brief moment, he was back in her arms. Back with Loreto. Back home in Mirabella.

But this time wasn't a dream. It wasn't an escape. He was home. His face was buried in Carmina's hair as he held on to her. And he only let go when a taller, older version of baby Loreto came sprinting to the front door where he and Carmina embraced. He dropped to one knee and caught the little girl that leapt into his arms, crying, telling him how much she loved him.

"Ti amo," he told her over and over. *I love you*.

That night, they had dinner as a family. Vico was so used to sitting around the table with Uncle Charlie and his family, but now he was back with his own. He found it difficult not to stop eating and simply stare at his wife and daughter who he hadn't seen in two years.

During dinner, they shared stories of one another's adventures. Loreto was so curious to know about America. Her young mind was so intrigued about the idea that there was another giant piece of land across the ocean and that Mirabella was just a tiny town in Italy. Vico described to her what the Statue of Liberty was like, how the train ride to Cleveland was, and how many Italians from the same area had found their way to live together in America. For his daughter, he left out the parts about the fourteen-day trip across the Atlantic that caused so many to become seasick. He left out the parts about the brutal conditions working in the foundry and how much he missed his girls back home.

For Loreto, the stories of his travels to a magical land that they could all one day call home were uplifting. Promising. He wanted his daughter to feel the level of excitement he felt for the possibility of a family trip to America. At night, when Loreto was asleep in her bed, he and Carmina shared more stories of the journey. He had written Carmina so many times that she knew of all his struggles, but he didn't know too many of hers. She wrote to him many times, but those letters mainly focused on Loreto and wondering how he was doing. So she let him know about what she had been doing to keep up the land and the sheep.

Vico was proud of his wife. She was a girl who had come from a home where she helped her mother bake, and then delivered those baked goods. She wasn't one who was accustomed to keeping up with farmland, yet she did an incredible job doing so. She was beautiful. And amazing. After they spoke, they extinguished the lamps in the house and went into bed. Vico and Carmina expressed just how much they truly missed each other's touch.

In the morning, when the sun rose and shone through the window, Vico woke and kissed his wife on the cheek. Then he walked to Loreto's room to do the same and rubbed his thumb across her forehead. He walked outside and stood on the front step of his home, looking out to the grassy hills of Mirabella and watched as the sun came over the horizon. It all felt like a dream. Being home, with Carmina and Loreto —it was what he saw in his dreams for two years. And now he was finally back.

But he didn't want to stay.

He knew he would soon remember the ongoing turmoil in his home country. The northern Italians looking down on him and his family would only push his desire to return to America and rid his wife and daughter of the embarrassment. He wanted a better life for them. As he looked out into the beautiful countryside of Italy, he thought he might one day miss it. But for now, he had to get his family across the Atlantic.

When Carmina and Loreto rose, they walked the grounds of their land as Carmina updated Vico on happenings since he had been gone. They tended to the sheep and their crops, and he consistently told his wife how well she did in his absence. And when he looked into her eyes, he thought he saw her pleading. She wanted to stay in Italy, but she knew he didn't.

There was no way. He had already paved the way for their trip with his two-year journey, and it would all be for nothing if they stayed. Their family would continue to be looked down upon, and the government would continue to ignore the financial struggles of southern Italy, as they had been ridiculed for doing in the years prior.

America was their escape. Vico knew it. So he spoke to his wife later in the day, when Loreto was off playing in the field, and told her. He promised her everything would work out. And she hesitantly agreed.

That day, it was made official: America would be their new home. Now they simply had to work on planning and getting the money to get the entire family to Cleveland.

CHAPTER 15

Several years had passed and Vico, Carmina, and Loreto were still living on the land Vico was given when his father died. Their plans for a move to America were taking much longer than anticipated. But they had to be right. He wouldn't allow himself to fail his family.

At the same time, Vico was growing impatient.

As time went on in Mirabella and weeks turned to months, months to years, Vico made sure to keep in touch with his Uncle Charlie in America. He was curious to know how everything was going. How the area was doing and whether or not more people were making their way across the Atlantic to a new home. What he really wanted to know was whether or not he would be able to find work once he got back to Cleveland.

August 1910
Dear Zia Charlie,
I hope all is well with you and your family
in Cleveland. I hope to return as soon as
I can but as you know my family is
growing and I have to carefully plan.
Are good jobs still open at Asher? Have
many paesani come from Campobasso?
I wish to come back as soon as I can. I
will write again when I can. My love to
Aunt Tomasina.
Your nephew, Vico

Vico was planning the trip back with his family with a lot more precision than when he'd first left. When it was just him and a bag over his shoulder, improvising wasn't so much a bad thing. If he needed to spend a night sleeping in some uncomfortable, outdoor area, it wasn't a big deal. But if his family had to do so too, that wouldn't be acceptable. And it wouldn't just be Carmina and Loreto anymore.

Their second daughter, Lena, was born two years after his return from America, which meant the trip would have to be pushed back even further than it already had been. And truth be told, it wasn't progressing fast enough to generate any sort of real target departure date.

While Vico anguished in the agony of not

knowing when he would be able to bring his family to Cleveland, his girls were just fine with their life in Italy. They were happy. Loreto was thrilled to be a big sister and helped Carmina to care for Lena. They loved to be out on the farm and roaming the lands of southern Italy, but the turmoil between the north and the south continued to grow, and Vico knew he needed to get his family away from it all.

In the early years after returning home, Vico would write to his Uncle Charlie as an act of kindness. He wanted to keep in touch, to see how Aunt Tomasina and the children were doing. To thank him for the hospitality he'd shown. But as the years went on, his letters grew more concerning. Uncle Charlie continued to tell him about the consistent growth in Cleveland and how more and more people from the old country were coming over in hopes of starting a new life. The news was never reassuring to Vico because he was concerned about finding a place to work in Cleveland if too many other Italians were getting there before him.

He was also growing impatient due to a looming war that would soon be called World War I. Italy's involvement in the war was yet to be known, but Vico didn't want to be stuck fighting for a country who wouldn't help to protect him and the other southern Italians.

On the other hand, he couldn't bring his family to America prematurely. Many Italians had emigrated to the U.S. too early, and the result was dismal. Without the proper planning, they were forced to come back home to Italy, and many were never able to go back to America again. Vico didn't want that. He didn't want to give his family hope of a new life just to be forced back onto a boat back home. He wanted to make sure everything would work out. That he, Carmina, and his two little girls would be okay there.

He continued to plan for years, and it wasn't until Loreto was eleven years old and Lena was five that Vico thought he was truly ready to make the journey. But even then, it wouldn't happen. Another road-block occurred when Carmina became pregnant. Plans had to change once again, and Vico knew he had to wait at least two more years before he could plan another trip. He knew Loreto and Lena were old enough when they were 11 and 5 that they could endure the journey, but with a newborn baby on the way, it wouldn't be possible.

In September of 1912, Carolina was born. The family was given a scare with a complicated birth and medical issues for Carmina that would cause her body to reject any future pregnancies. But she was alive and well, and although they couldn't grow their family any larger, Vico was happy with his family of girls. He wanted to protect them. To give them a good life. And so he improvised.

When Carolina was born in 1912, it had been six

years since Vico was living in America. It was a long gap—far longer than he imagined when he returned home to Italy after being there for two years—and he knew he couldn't wait much longer. He and Carmina would speak on occasion about what their next steps would be, but it always resulted in them looking over at baby Carolina in her bassinet, wrapped up in warm blankets. She was too young to take on a trip across the ocean.

Carmina was afraid to leave, and Vico could tell. As much as he continued to reassure her that going to America would be a good thing, she had her doubts. Although he told her about all the Italians in Cleveland and how they still spoke Italian while living in America, Carmina couldn't wrap her head around a new home outside of Italy.

Suddenly, months went by. And then it had been another year and still no progress was made on their trip. No plan in place. No promise of leaving anytime soon. More letters came in from Uncle Charlie telling Vico about the consistent growth of the area's population and the number of people finding jobs at Asher Metalworks.

Vico was making money for his family by selling his farm's product at the local market. He would barter some, and sometimes he would be paid. The pay wasn't much—not nearly what he knew he could make in America—but it was enough to start saving if he needed to. In 1913, he made a plan to save up money until he could afford to get himself to America, then he would go back to Cleveland, work for one year, and then he would use that money to bring his family over to the U.S.

He could see in Carmina's eyes when he told her about the plan that she didn't want him to leave again. She nodded when he told her, but her eyes watered and the look she gave him was a pleading one. It was asking him to stay. To just be okay with Italy as their home and to let the family run the farm and one day hand it over to the girls. But the land wasn't good enough. It was the reason his brother wanted nothing to do with it and decided to travel elsewhere for work. Vico knew he couldn't keep the land just to hand it over to a man who would eventually marry one of his daughters. It would simply continue a trend of trying to maintain land that wasn't ideal for producing. America, on the other hand, gave them a world of opportunity to be free and to provide a better future for the girls.

Vico was able to spend another year with his family, and then on October 4th of 1914, he laid his head down on his bed beside Carmina for what would once again be the last time in a long while. The last time they had been with each other in this situation, they were both younger. They only had one child, and it tore Vico's heart to pieces to think he'd be away from her for so long. And now there were three little girls. Plus Carmina. It killed Vico to think about being away from them for so long, but this was a dilemma for so many Italian men of the time. He knew he wasn't alone. And he was being selfish if he stayed home to watch his daughters grow. Because staying home to watch them grow meant watching them grow in Italy, ridiculed for their status and being embarrassed for their entire life. Leaving them would be tough, but it would be better for his daughters in the long run.

Or so he thought. Time would determine this to be completely untrue. But in the moment, Vico could have never known the pain his girls would endure.

CHAPTER 16

*C*armina looked into the closed, sleeping eyes of her husband. Vico had always been a hard-working man, but he was also a man who continually stressed over the idea of living in America. To Carmina, their lives in Italy were just fine. They had a simple life, sure, but they didn't need much. She could bake and Vico could tend to the land. They could sell what they produced and make a nice living for their family. The girls could grow up learning to bake just as she had with her mother.

Vico wouldn't let go of the idea of America, though. And now here they were, lying close and dreading the sunrise that would be his cue to leave for the shipyard of Naples again. The only difference is that this time, Carmina would be left to care for three kids as well as the land and the animals. More importantly, she would be left in an empty bed once again.

Regardless of the situation, she wasn't upset with him. She knew where his mindset was. And she, too, was aware of the war that had broken out just a few months prior. Italy was part of a Triple Alliance with Germany and Austria-Hungary, and the two were some of the first participants in the war. Italy, being part of the alliance, was disrespecting the Triple Alliance by not joining the war immediately, but it had saved Vico and many other countrymen from having to fight. For that, Carmina was thankful. But she also knew that Vico could be called at any time to join, so his trip to America could have some upside. She just hated to see him go. Again.

In the morning, when the sun rose, she prepared herself to see her husband off. This time, Loreto was by her side while Lena and Carolina remained asleep. Carmina and her oldest daughter stood side by side as they watched Vico walk off in the distance, over the grassy hill and out of sight. Neither cried. Carmina could only imagine her daughter's level of despair, but she, too, knew how close her father could come to being forced into the war. Perhaps she was happier to see her father head off to the land of opportunity than to a land distraught by war and gunfire.

With Vico gone, Carmina was forced to go on with life as usual back in Italy. Somehow, she had no sense of excitement for his anticipated return—or for their departure to meet him in America. During his previous trip, she found herself thinking of him often, wondering how he was doing and where he was. But in this instance, she couldn't bring herself to do it. At the same time, she couldn't bring herself to be happy. She couldn't smile. Couldn't think of anything but the loneliness she'd been left with. The girls all had each other and were growing up together, playing outside and learning to maintain the land. But Carmina was left alone. She would seek help from her girls in the kitchen when she needed it and teach them about baking, but that was all she had. Teach the kids, cook for them, maintain the land. It had been her only purpose in life for so many years, and she was growing tired of it.

November 1914
Dear Carmina,
I have arrived safe in America after going
    thru all immigration procedures once
    more. The Statue of Liberty was just as
    beautiful this second time, and can't
    wait for you to see her. I am back at
    Mrs. Carlucci's and have a roommate
    named Pietro Giullani who has a
    brother named Mario who helps with
    many tasks here in Cleveland. My old

> job at Asher was still available and I
> was happy to accept it. The harder I
> work the sooner you can come over.
> Love, Vico

Vico still sent letters and she would still respond. Their communication never stopped. He would tell her about his tough days, and she would write back about how great the girls were doing. Even though the conversations didn't change much, they still sent letters often. They still spoke. Vico would show his excitement at how close they were to having their American Dream, and Carmina would pretend to share. Somehow, though, she could never picture the image. She could never see herself going on the voyage to America. For whatever reason, she couldn't get excited for it.

> February 1915
> Dear Vico,
> Once again you are gone and I miss you so
> much. Your girls are such good helpers
> but also miss you. Little Carolina looks
> for you each day. Lena is growing up
> fast and is a great help to Loreto. Your
> oldest daughter is becoming a beautiful
> young woman and will make you proud

when we come to America. Be safe my
husband and know that we think of you
each day.
  Love, Carmina

Several months after Vico left, Carmina found herself getting sick quite often. She would grow tired easily and couldn't handle days on the farm the way she used to. Luckily, she had her girls with her, and Loreto was incredibly helpful. She was 12 going on 13, but she acted like the selfless young woman she would grow up to be, although Carmina had no idea the extent Loreto would need to go.

Her sickness led her to finally see a doctor. As the only one there to watch over the girls, Carmina knew she had to get the necessary help to keep her healthy and able to care for her family.

Dr. Portofino was an elderly man, short in stature, and when he walked down the path toward the front of the house, Carmina saw the curiosity in her daughters' eyes. Loreto was old enough to know that he was there to check up on their mother, but Lena had many questions to ask and Carolina was too young to know what was going on. Still, Carmina watched as the three of them stood still in the middle of the grassy field and watched as the man entered their house for the first time.

"Hai un cuore cattivo," Dr. Portofino said to her after an examination.

A bad heart? she replied back to him in her native, Italian tongue. She wondered how that could be. She was growing older, nearing her mid-30s which, for 1914, was middle-aged. But she wasn't old enough to where she would have such severe, chronic problems.

Carmina and her doctor spoke, and he informed her that she would need to bring some joy into her life. Her heart was literally breaking. And when they discussed a possible cause for her failing heart, the only explanation was Vico.

As a young woman, Carmina had been through so much. She had lost Antonio, the man she thought would be her love, at an early age. And then she was forced to move away from the beautiful Italian seaside and into a small plot of land Vico's father had left him. She had given birth to three children and spent so many years of her adult life alone while Vico was in America. It wasn't the life she saw herself having when she was younger. Her parents remained in their small town for her entire childhood. Her father was home every night and her mother was always there for her. That was the life she expected her own children to have. But Vico's desire to go to America had interfered with it. It had caused her to be lonely. In need of some companionship and able to have none.

Though she had birthed three children and

tending to the land had caused her hands to become calloused, she was still an attractive woman and she still had her opportunities for companionship. But as a woman faithful to her husband, she never acted. She knew Vico's heart was in the right place with his intent to bring his family to America and although it left her lonely and depressed, she couldn't hurt him by bedding another man.

As Dr. Portofino made his way out the door, he informed Carmina that there was no medicine available for her condition. In 1914, the pharmaceutical industry was blossoming, but there had been no medication to treat a failing heart. These were the times where cigarette smoking was said to be beneficial to the lungs and, although Dr. Portofino couldn't have known the science that would come years later, he was one of the doctors who had supported this idea.

"Grazie," Carmina said to Dr. Portofino as he left with his top hat on and his briefcase by his side. Her girls looked over at her, and she smiled back. She knew they needed her and she needed them just as much. Without their love, her heart might have given out already. Certainly, she wouldn't have been able to handle life on her own for all this time if she hadn't had children whom she could love and adore.

Later that night, while passing bowls of food to one another at the wooden dinner table, her daughters had asked her about the doctor's visit.

Is something wrong?

Why was he here?

But she wouldn't let her daughters know about her medical condition. Her job was to make sure the girls were happy and kept safe until they could make their trip to America.

This trip of Vico's was only set to be one year. Several months had already passed, and it was only a matter of time before he made enough money to buy and send home tickets for the four of them to get on a ship across the Atlantic. Carmina told herself she could hold out. Less than one year and then she could be with her beloved Vico again. She would no longer need to tend to the land nor would she have to look at pictures of her husband and pray for his return to her arms. In less than one year's time, she would be able to be in America with him and the girls. Life would be the way she had expected it to be. She would be home during the day, teaching the girls to read, write, cook, and clean. And Vico would work during the day and then come home at night. No more turmoil tearing apart their country. No more being ridiculed by the northern Italians for being a poor, southern Italian. Once in America, they would simply be Americans. That was all Vico ever wanted and soon he would have his dream.

This is what Carmina told herself that night as she placed her head on her pillow, extinguished the lamp by her side and closed her eyes to go to sleep.

CHAPTER 17

*V*ico's main priority was to save money. The faster he saved his money, the faster he could bring his family to America. This had been the dream of his since he met Carmina: to have a family in America where they could be free from ridicule. And Cleveland was home to so many Italians—it would feel as if they had never left.

Vico was back in Mrs. Carlluci's place, sharing a room with a man named Pietro for three dollars per week. Once his family came over, he wouldn't be able to stay in the boarding house any longer. He would need to get his own place. He knew this would take time, and he was thankful to his Uncle Charlie who agreed that, once Carmina and the girls were here, they could all stay at his house. Vico would, of course, need to chip in financially, but he was okay with that. Happy to do so. He would have his family with him and that's all he wanted.

Asher Metalworks had grown since he last worked there years prior. The foundry had grown in size as had the crew of men working inside the hot and muggy building. There were also more people living in the Cleveland area and many more stores were open. There was much more for the locals to do now than there had been nearly a decade before. One of the local hot spots—especially for the workers of Asher Metalworks—was a place called Grotto Bar. Many of the men who were in America to work and save were regulars to the bar. Some blew all their money and never saved enough for their families. They ended up leaving the country with their head hung low, regretting their decision to indulge in the delights of one too many beers on common occasion.

Vico was sure to avoid being one of these men. After all, he was a man in his mid-thirties and many of the young men coming over were just entering adulthood. He had a wife and three children at home and needed to get them tickets to travel as soon as he could. Each penny counted when it came to this.

That being said, he still liked to blow off some steam every now and then while sitting on a wooden stool and drinking a pint or two on his way home from a long day of work. He'd grown accustomed to the men who gathered in the bar. Antonio DiPalma was one of those men. He made the move to America in 1914 and had a wife and children back home in Sicily that he was attempting to bring over. Mario Giuliani was another. Mario was the brother of Pietro, Vico's roommate at the boarding house. He was a man who had a reputation of getting things done when asked of him. It would be a trait Vico would seek out in him in the near future.

Though Vico wasn't at the bar as often as many others, he still grew accustomed to seeing the bar's owner, Tony Musso, who was a gruff and tough owner if there ever was one. He was a burly man, tall for an Italian, and had a no-nonsense attitude. His main bartender, Julia Torolli, was his counter opposite. She was always smiling, keeping the customers upbeat and happy. Although there were plenty of fights in the bar—ironically enough, they were over Julia—she brought a sense of joy into the place.

Julia was tan-skinned and had blazing blue eyes that many northern Italians possessed. She was extremely attractive and caught the eye of nearly every man that walked through the doors of Grotto Bar. And for some reason, she gave Vico special attention.

Maybe it was because he wasn't like the other men who came into the bar. He wasn't a regular and when he *was* in the bar, he wasn't drunk. He came to blow off steam, have a drink or two and head back to the boarding house to clean up and get ready for another day of work. To him, making each day go by faster meant he was able to see his family sooner. So the thought of spending his money at the bar was counterproductive to what he was trying to accomplish.

Julia gave him more attention than the other men who would hang over the bar. It upset some of the patrons who had put in so much time and energy into getting her to speak to them, and when she would favor Vico's conversation over their own, some of the men who had too much to drink would shoot him stares or yell across the room. One night, he was confronted by two men and that's when he left. He told Julia he'd be back another day and he went off, back to Mrs. Carlluci's house on 126th Street.

After that night, Vico was hesitant to return to Grotto Bar. The hostility toward him was getting worse and he had no desire to get into trouble over Julia. His heart was back in Mirabella with Carmina.

The next few nights after work, he happily walked past the bar on his way to the boarding house where he'd clean up, have dinner, and call it a night. But as he walked past the bar, the noise from inside grew and he looked over to see the door swing open. Julia was running out and stopped to talk to him. As was the case almost everywhere in Cleveland, she spoke in Italian and asked him, "Where have you been?"

"Just trying to avoid getting my face kicked in," he said with a smile.

She tried to lure Vico inside with a pint on her, but he declined. And when her flirtatious smiles and offers for free beer went unclaimed, she reluctantly let him go.

"I'm off on Thursdays," she said before she walked back. "I live right down the block," she pointed. "Let's have a drink at my place sometime. I promise, no one will be there to kick your face in." And then she was inside the bar again as the door swung shut on its hinges.

Vico was left in the street to wonder how he'd managed to capture the attention of this beautiful young woman. She was in her early twenties, and he was a man more than a decade older. She had her choice of men in the bar and yet she chased the one man who steered clear of the place. He walked back to Mrs. Carlluci's place that night and put his head on the pillow. On the other side of the room was Pietro, whose brother was a local to the bar, and he was tempted to ask Pietro if Mario had ever mentioned Julia being this way with anyone else. But he decided to let it go. Carmina was his and he was Carmina's. There would be no gathering on any Thursday. He was in America to work and that was it.

When the next Thursday came, he could barely focus at work. Vico had been a faithful man his entire life and he wasn't ready to change that, but he was still in awe at Julia's attraction to him. He wondered what it could have possibly been. And he wondered how he would explain to her the reason for his declining her invitation for a drink at her place. Surely, she wasn't used to being turned down by men. This must have been just as new to her as being admired was new to Vico.

He walked by the entrance to Grotto Bar that night on his way home from work and heard the muffled noise of loud, drunken chatter. He knew Julia wasn't in there—that she was in her home somewhere down the street where she had pointed to him several nights before. As he continued down the quiet street, the dusk sky hung over the city leaving a tired and restful blanket over its inhabitants. Vico was ready to get back to the boarding house and wash up. He was hungry. Thirsty. And ready to end this day and get to the next—one day closer to seeing his family. He was considering even taking the time to write to Carmina and the girls if he could get in the writing before the sun set completely, leaving Mrs. Carlluci's house relatively dark.

"Ciao," he heard the voice call. And although it was familiar, it still startled him.

Julia giggled and apologized for scaring him and then she held up a bottle of red wine. "From the old country," she said in her native language. "Can I pour you a glass?"

She was stunning. The clothes she wore while sitting inside her home were so much more revealing than the outfit she wore to tend bar. It was as if she'd planned it. And maybe she had. Who was he kidding? Of course she had. Now he was simply being naïve. She was trying to lure him into her place, and he was trying so hard to fight the urge but the word came out of his mouth so naturally.

"Sì," he said. *Yes*. And then some unnatural force started pulling him in her direction. She led him up a set of stairs and into a doorway. As she walked, he felt like he was losing his ability to control himself. He was trying so hard to be loyal to Carmina back home and keep his eyes off of her, but her figure was beautiful. Each day of his was spent inside the foundry with sweaty men, and he hadn't seen his wife in months. Being able to talk to Julia while at Grotto Bar was nice, but this was an entirely new level of intimacy. He was alone with her. Following her into where she lived. Where her bed was. Where she bathed. Changed. Got herself ready for a shift at the bar. It was her place of comfort and she was inviting Vico into it. To be part of it.

Once inside her home, they were in the kitchen and she poured two glasses of red wine. She handed Vico his with a smile that was like a dagger to his heart. He was so torn that it hurt. As she put the glass to her lips, he followed.

They talked for a while, just as they did when at the bar. Then they moved from the kitchen to the couch, and as the conversation became deeper—talking about the old country, travels across the Atlantic, and loneliness—Julia continued to move closer to him.

And then he caved. Everything in his mind disappeared. He relaxed. He stopped being timid. He stopped fighting it. He allowed himself to take in this moment that nearly every man in Cleveland would kill to be involved in. And he felt no regret towards it. The goal of coming to America was to help his family and he had sacrificed nearly half of his life to ensure they all would have a better future.

She sensed it. The second he let down his guard, she pounced on the opportunity. Julia sat up, swung one leg over Vico's lap and straddled him, looked down, smiled, and bit her lip. And from there, all he could do was admire the beauty before him as it began to reveal itself.

CHAPTER 18

*I*t seemed like only a minute ago that he'd been walking *up* the stairs leading to Julia's place, admiring her beauty. Her figure. Everything he missed about Carmina and desired to have again. And now he was walking *down*. His shoulders were slouched. His head down. His heart hurt. What had he done?

The guilt was unbearable. With each downward step he took, he felt like he was walking one step closer to a reality he didn't want. When he finally hit the bottom of the staircase, he walked out and into the dark, lonely street. He didn't stop walking until he reached Mrs. Carlucci's house and once there, he walked into his room, put his head on his pillow, and wished he would wake up to find this was all a dream. A good dream and a bad dream all in one. But a dream nonetheless. Because a dream would mean he didn't really follow Julia up the steps to her place. And he didn't betray the trust of his wife. The same wife who he was working so hard for, to allow her to come to be with him.

That night, he barely slept. His roommate, Pietro, snored and slept soundly. Vico listened to him. Despised him. Despised his peacefulness. But really, he simply hated himself.

Why do this? Why struggle for years and years to try to make the move to America work when he couldn't control himself? He was better than the other men who lost their wives and families back home. He continually told himself that. That he was a good man. An honorable man. A hard worker who was sacrificing a peaceful life in order to set up his wife and daughters for a better future.

But he was no different. During both of his trips to America and his time working at Asher Metal-works, he was *proud* of what he was able to avoid. He was *proud* he didn't spend his nights sitting atop a barstool, throwing money toward a habit that would only delay his family from coming here. That he was being a responsible husband and father and doing everything in his power to not indulge in any leisurely activities until his family was there with him.

And in one night—in one *hour*—that was ruined.

When the sun rose and the light poured through the windows of his bedroom, Vico's eyes were open.

He slept here and there throughout the night, but not enough. Not enough to prepare him for the grueling workday ahead.

Regardless, he had to wake up. He had to get going. Each hour he worked brought him one hour closer to seeing his family. And that was all he wanted. It pained him to think about them. They had no idea what he was doing and he had no idea what *they* were doing. Nothing about their lives was in sync. They were tending to a farm and he was in some sweat shop. He was alone and they had each other. Even their days were different—the six-hour time difference meant when he was starting his workday, they were getting ready to end theirs.

Vico needed them. He wanted them there so he wouldn't be lonely anymore. He knew his affair with Julia was a mistake and the only way he could get their lives back to normal was to bring Carmina and the girls to America. So he didn't allow himself to think about Julia anymore. Or about a quick drink after work at Grotto Bar. He worked. That was all he cared about. Working to save money so he could have his family back.

Days went by, and then a few weeks. Each night after work, he would listen to the mumbled chatter that would take place on the other side of the entrance to Grotto Bar but never had the urge to go in. For so long, he looked down upon the men who went there every day, salivating over the opportunity to talk to the beautiful bartender. Vico thought of those men and what their wives at home would think of them being so blatantly aggressive with her. He thought that his level-headedness made him better than them. It meant he could control himself and his urges better.

In the end, he realized he was no better than them. Worse, even. He had done what they all desired to do but in the end, never did. Flirt or not, they never went through with the unfaithful act.

Every night he heard the chatter, but he would walk right on by. He would have dinner with Uncle Charlie and his family and then head back to Mrs. Carlluci's for bed, ready to wake up the next day and start all over. He would allow himself no more moments of joy until his family was with him.

On one of the nights where Vico was tossing and turning on his mattress, exhausted from a hard day's worth of work but still unable to sleep, the voice of his roommate Pietro startled him.

"Sorry," Pietro said in his native tongue. "I was just thinking about something. Do you have a plan for your family to come here yet?"

He didn't. He was working and waiting until he had enough money saved to buy steerage tickets for Carmina and the girls but other than that, the details were still yet to be planned out. Getting them from the family home in Campobasso to the Naples ship-yard was still not in order.

Cleveland was home to many Italian immigrants, most of whom came from the same areas of Italy. So they looked out for one another. Ties of family and friends remained close, although they were thousands of miles apart. One of the common acts displayed was in protecting one's family who was about to make the journey to America.

In the case of Italians coming to America, Vico's situation was common. The man of the house would emigrate first in order to start working and preserve enough money to begin a life. Then, he would send tickets for his family to come over once he was able to. And some men made their money off of overseeing these journeys. Pietro had let Vico know that his brother was one of them.

The last time Vico saw Pietro's brother, Mario, it was slouched on a barstool at Grotto Bar. He was a local, and it often amazed Vico how he could be there so often, spending money. And now he knew where he got it. He was overseeing the trips of families to the new country and charging a decent price for doing so. As Vico laid in the dark, he listened to Pietro describe what it was his brother did and how he was available if Vico needed him.

It was a hefty price to pay, but if it meant his wife and daughters would have protection throughout the travel process, it was worth it. Vico remembered his own trips and how brutal they were. How crowded and chaotic. He found it difficult to manage on his own, and he couldn't imagine doing so with three daughters with him. Carmina was bound to be in for a rough few weeks during the trip, and if he could pay someone $100 to alleviate some of her pain during the trip, he would happily do so.

It took him a bit more time to work and make the extra $100, but once he did and he had enough money saved to buy the tickets for Carmina and the girls, he felt safer knowing they would be watched over. He felt safe knowing that while his girls were fighting crowds of steerage passengers traveling across the Atlantic, that they wouldn't be alone. Or when they walked the grand staircase of Great Hall for their examinations, they wouldn't be nervous because they would have someone with them to explain everything.

Overall, he felt the $100 investment was one that would be best for his family.

When the time came and he had the money, he bought the tickets and sent them home to Carmina and the girls. And then he paid Mario for the services he would offer.

May 1915
Dear Carmina,
We are so close now to all being together in
America. I am sending you tickets for
you and the girls to travel to America. I

have also employed a man named
Mario Giuliani who will meet you in
Mirabella and guide you all the way to
Cleveland. My heart is so full as I wait
to see you and my daughters in
America.

Love, Vico

It was finally happening. Vico was bringing his family to America. No more hostility in Italy. No more being belittled by the northerners, and no more hard labor for Carmina on the land. *All* of his girls would have a better life in America.

And with the purchase of Mario Giuliani's services, they would get off to a great start.

Or so he thought.

PART III
THE SISTERS

CHAPTER 19

*H*er father's life had been anything but ordinary. Loreto could remember as if it was yesterday, her father coming home from his first trip to America. "Vico!" She could hear her mother's muffled voice coming from the front door of their home. Her shriek sent a shock wave down Loreto's spine.

Loreto was young when that happened—a girl of only six years old. She was now a sixteen-year-old girl playing the role of supporting mother to her two younger sisters. And she could play the part well. She was as tall as her mother now with long, black hair to match. Her olive skin and brown eyes matched both her mother's and her father's.

Lena was eight and Carolina was only three. Still so young and innocent, Loreto would tell herself. And they now had tickets to board a ship that would take them several thousand miles away, to their new life in America.

A new life in America. Loreto had heard her parents talk about it so often. She could see the spark in her father's eye whenever he would talk about it. That spark never seemed to ignite in her mother's. There was some daughterly intuition there that told her she didn't want to go. As much as her father wanted to join the hundreds of thousands of Italians who found a better life in America, her mother never felt the same sense of optimism that life would be better.

Regardless, even during the times when her father was gone, working in America, her mother never belittled the idea. Not in front of Loreto, at least. She encouraged her husband's desire.

Today was the day her father had talked about so often. They were leaving. Dad had sent a man named Mario who came to the house the day before to talk to Loreto and Carmina about the trip while Lena and Carolina played in the field. He explained the train rides across the Italian countryside, the boat ride and the crowded conditions that would come with it, and the subsequent travels once in America. And now, they simply waited for him to arrive to take them on the journey.

Loreto waited in the kitchen with the other girls as their mother sought Dr. Portofino's advice one last time. When they came out of the bedroom, both had looks on their faces as if they'd known a conversation was coming and couldn't relay it. As if something was on the tip of their tongue for so long yet they couldn't say a thing until now.

"Loreto," her mother called to her quietly. "Lasciami parlare con te." *Let me speak with you.*

Loreto was pulled aside by her mother who informed her that she was sick. There were frequent visits from Dr. Portofino over the previous months, and, as a sixteen-year-old, Loreto knew something wasn't right. But she carried on without prying too far into her mother's arrangements, fearful that she may learn something she didn't want to. But her mother knew that Loreto, as a young woman now—old enough to be wed, old enough to bear children of her own—could handle the news.

I cannot make the trip, she told Loreto. *I am too sick. Dr. Portofino says I must rest. You must care for the girls.*

Dad's choice to send Mario as a helping hand was the only way her mother would have allowed for this and Loreto knew it. Was her mother really sick? And had her father known about it? Was that why he sent Mario?

The news floored young Loreto. She was crushed. She had known nothing but life with her mother. Never went a single day without her mother's presence. And now, on the morning they had plans to leave for a three-week journey to another country, her mother had let her know she couldn't go. Her weakening heart wouldn't be able to withstand the journey, according to Dr. Portofino. *But he said I should be okay in just a few weeks*, her mother had told her. *And I'll be there as soon as I can.*

Loreto had to stand by her mother's side as she informed Lena and Carolina. While Carolina had no reaction—at three years old, she was too young to realize what this meant—Lena's reaction was to look up, wide-eyed at her big sister as if to say *Do we really have to do this alone?*

They would be fine. Loreto was sure of it. She had seen girls her age who were married and with children when she went to the market. She knew her time would soon come and that she was perfectly capable of caring for her younger sisters. This journey was something that would help the entire family, and if they had sent word back to their father that none would be coming due to mother's illness, he would be devastated. All of his hard work and planning over the years would be for nothing.

I'll write your father, Carmina said to her girls. By doing this, the excitement of seeing his girls wouldn't be overshadowed by the unexpected news that his wife had not come along on the trip. For this, Loreto was happy. She, too, wanted the first moments with her father in America to be special.

April 1915
Dear Vico,

My heart is breaking as I write you this letter. First I had to see my children leave me to make the long journey to you. The tears I shed were both of joy and sorrow for my daughters. I am happy to know they will be in America with their father and a bright future. At the same time life without them close will be hard. I hope you have received this letter before their arrival in Cleveland. I have had some troubling issues with my heart and Dr. Portofino suggested I should not make the trip at this time. I will come later. Please take care of my darlings and yourself.

Love, Carmina

Loreto and her sisters spent the little time they had left with their mother exchanging hugs and shedding tears. Soon after they heard the news that she wouldn't be coming, Mario arrived and was ready to begin his voyage to America with the family of the man that had paid him $100 to do so.

Loreto had to help reassure Lena that it would only be a few short weeks until they saw their mother again, and it would be in America. Where their family would be happily settled. She told Lena that they would be able to figure out the best spots for Mom to bake and sell her goods by the time she arrived. And that they would make friends with others in the town and help to acclimate her to her new home when she *did* arrive. Still too young to realize the extent of what was happening, Carolina simply looked forward to the train and boat rides.

Fog had hung low in Mirabella on the morning Mario led the girls off to their journey to America. Their mother had watched from the door, and Loreto remembered how she did the same thing twice before, watching her beloved Vico leave. Now she stood in the doorway and in the house behind, there would be no one. She wouldn't have daughters to turn to this time, to hug, and to help her get through the difficult nights. As Loreto looked back at her mother, she could only imagine the loneliness she would feel until she was given permission to be able to travel.

Water filled Carmina's eyes and Loreto tried as hard as she could to keep her composure. She needed to be strong for her sisters. She needed to swallow the lump in her throat, so she gave one last nod to her mother and turned to her sisters and Mario up ahead. Each had a bag with them. Even Carolina, with her small bag fitting only the most important things she would need for the trip.

The girls made their way up the grassy hill of their farm, and when the hill began to descend when they were on the other side, Loreto looked for one of her sisters to turn one last time to their mother but neither did. So she felt compelled not to either. They continued walking through the misty Italian morning toward the train station several kilometers away where they would begin their first leg of the journey.

Mario had kept a quick pace during the walk and ensured the girls that they would need to do so as well. His manner wasn't harsh, but it sure wasn't friendly. He was a man with a job and that was all. There was no emotion or empathy behind his words.

As they boarded the train and loaded their bags, Mario was helpful in ensuring each girl got into their seat and their bags were on board as well. But other than that, the ride was quiet. Mario remained seated forward and his only movements were the ones the train had caused. He had greasy, brown hair hanging down beneath a fedora that jumped each time the train would rock. In times when he seemed bored, Loreto would see hum fuss with his mustache. He was a quiet man—a man on a mission, she supposed.

Loreto sat with her sisters as the train moved along. Lena and Carolina would fall in and out of sleep during the hours-long trip and as the acting mother of these two little girls, Loreto forced her eyes to remain open. She needed to look out for them. She was only a few hours into what would become a life of this guardianship mentality over her sisters.

CHAPTER 20

The train began to slow as they approached Naples. Loreto had to wake Lena from sleeping on her shoulder, but Carolina was already looking out the window in awe. In front of them, hard to see from the angle of the train but still more visible than not, was the Naples shipyard.

As the train squealed to a halt and passengers began to disembark, the girls grabbed their belongings and followed Mario's orders. He was kind enough to take the bags of Loreto and Carolina, which allowed Loreto to carry her little sister through the crowded station and out to an even more crowded shipyard.

The site was like nothing the girls had ever seen before. Massive ships were lined along the edge of the water and past them, nothing but a giant, blue body of water that seemed to stretch forever. It was the Bay of Naples she had heard so much about. During her years, Loreto had made the trip with her mother to visit her grandparents in Termoli, but that small body of water off the coastal town was nothing like this.

Mario led them across a path to where an open bench sat by the water's edge. He sat them down and set their briefcases behind them, then told Loreto he would be right back. He needed to speak with someone to figure out when boarding of the ship would begin.

Loreto found the level of excitement growing inside of her. She would certainly miss her home in Italy and the fact that her mother wasn't along for this trip made it even more difficult, but she and her sisters were about to move to America. It was the country all Italians were talking about at the time. One of promise. Of hope. Where her father would be able to provide a better life for them all. It wouldn't feel whole until their mother was with them again, but as she and Dr. Portofino had said, it wouldn't be too long.

When Mario returned, he let the girls know it would be another few hours before boarding began. It would begin at 8:00 and the ship would depart a few hours after, at midnight.

Those few hours leading up to 8:00 were long, but the time finally came and the girls followed Mario— who was carrying the bags once again—toward the ship. The sun was setting in the sky behind them as they approached, and it made the reflection off the water around the ship a dark orange. But it was the massive size of the ship, and not the beautiful sunset, that consumed their attention.

They stood in a line that inched forward as passengers in front of them boarded. The girls followed close behind Mario as he walked along a thin ramp that sent them upward and toward the ship's entrance. It was a wobbly thing but with ropes as handrails, they were all able to remain steady. And they waited their turn and inched along the moving line until they were all standing in front of two men wearing identical hats that looked to Loreto like something men in the army would wear to a ball. They collected the tickets handed to them by Mario and took the names of all four passengers before allowing them to walk on board.

And then they were in. The girls were on board the ship that would take them to see their father. For a second, Loreto was saddened by the thought of potentially never stepping foot on Italian soil again, but she wasn't completely sure she wouldn't. There were ships coming back all the time and even if she wasn't coming back for good, she thought to herself that she could come back to visit.

She allowed herself instead to be amazed by the large, upper deck of the ship and all the people walking around. But they all looked so fancy. So rich.

Yet Loreto and her sisters were not. And they would soon find out that the upper deck wasn't for them. And the reason for their path being roped off was so no steerage passengers could sneak their way onto the deck and into first-class accommodations.

Regardless of where they were on the ship, Loreto whispered to her sisters to be happy and that they would soon be in America with their father. She wouldn't be disappointed in what her father was able to afford in the way of their travel arrangements and certainly wouldn't be ungrateful.

But that mindset changed somewhat as the steerage passengers made their way down a few flights of stairs and into their own living quarters, where there were no large, outside decks. There were instead white walls with white doors and gray floors. Worse was the news she was about to hear from Mario.

After hitting the steerage floor and walking down a few hallways with the girls, Mario stopped and set the girls' bags he was holding on the floor next to a bench. People bustled by in both directions, both happy and frantic. The pace down below was nowhere near as calm and relaxed as it was in the deck above. And the panic that would set in with Loreto and the girls would soon add to it.

I'm in second-class, Mario told them. *I won't be staying here with you.*

"Che cosa?" *What?*

After a brief explanation of where they could find their accommodations and food during the trip, he was gone. He said he would be back to check on them every day and then he was off. Heading back toward the stairwell, leaving sixteen-year-old Loreto to fend for herself and her two younger sisters. They stood by the bench and people continued to hustle by, bumping into them and their bags on the ground. It was clear that Loreto would have no help or empathy from passersby after what had just happened. She was the only one who would be able to act, so she did. She had to put down Carolina and pick up the bags and she took them, with her sisters walking behind her, to the accommodations set up for women only. There were sections for men only, women only, and families, and while she could have taken them to the family quarters, she felt much safer in women only.

And it was there that they found places to lie their heads. Bunks were stacked two high and she picked out three of them for her and her sisters. Inside the room and out in the halls, the ship was still buzzing with excitement and anxiousness from the passengers but on those three beds, things were a bit still. The girls were tired. From her top bunk, Loreto could look down to check on Lena and Carolina at any point in the night and on occasion, she did. Especially when she could feel the ship start to move. People cheered and Loreto could hear running feet stomping across the hallways outside the women's quarters.

She allowed herself to smile and looked down to see if her sisters were awake. But they weren't. They were both sleeping, tired from their travels. So she allowed herself to rest her head on the pillow, close her eyes, and feel the light rocking of the boat as it made its way out of the Bay of Naples and into the vast ocean. She thought about what it must look like from the outside, a large ship like this cutting through the calm, dark waters of the night ocean. She thought about what could possibly lie beneath the surface of the ocean and how amazing it was that a boat this size and with all these people on it could float.

And those thoughts made her smile. They carried on, with Loreto wondering how all this worked, until all went black and she was sound asleep.

CHAPTER 21

here never seemed to be a time when the ship was completely quiet. Maybe it was the first night's excitement or the fact that there were too many people on board—in the women's quarters especially—to have everyone sleep at once.

Throughout the course of the night, Loreto found herself in and out of sleep. And she found herself looking over the edge of her bed and down onto her sisters each time her eyes slipped open. She would find that they were okay, sound asleep and comfortable. Still, she couldn't find herself able to sleep through the night. And in the morning, when the children within the large sleeping quarters began to rise, so too did everyone else.

After taking the girls to the facilities to wash up, Loreto led them to the dining room where they would have oatmeal porridge and toast for breakfast.

It was different from what they were used to at home so the girls were happy about it. Loreto, on the other hand, was simply happy that they were able to eat. Mario had yet to come down to check on them, and she had no idea what they should do for the remainder of the trip.

While in the dining hall, she overheard families talking about the observation deck in the rear. Loreto wondered if it was something like she saw when they first walked onto the ship—a vast, open space with beautiful wooden planks lining the floor. She could only imagine the beautiful view now, as they were making their way across the ocean. After breakfast, Loreto took the girls and followed behind the family speaking of the observation deck, and they were led right to it.

The observation deck for steerage passengers wasn't nearly what had been built for first-class. It was much smaller and hung off the back of the ship. But it still gave a view of the ocean—something new to them. Loreto and the girls leaned over the railing and saw a streak of white, frothy water pushing out from beneath the ship and extending for what looked like miles. It was as if that white line could lead them right back home. Back to mother. And it was at that moment that Loreto grabbed her sisters tight and tears began to run down her face.

They were in the middle of nowhere. In an ocean where neither parent was even close. None could come help if called. And they were still more than two weeks away from hitting dry land again.

Thick, black smoke hung in the air overtop the line of white, frothy water and Loreto had no idea where it came from. She would learn that it was from the steam engines down below, pushing out through the cylinder stacks rising out of the ship's interior. Staying on the observation deck for too long meant letting the smoke cover you. And since she and the girls had already washed up for the morning, she preferred they not be covered in filth. They went back down into the congested living space and occupied their time by playing games and telling stories. And then when dinner came, they headed to the dining hall once more for tomato soup and bread. It filled their stomachs enough to allow even Loreto to sleep through the night.

The next morning was oatmeal porridge and toast again and for dinner that night, more soup and bread. It was all the girls would be served during the trip, and it became fairly tasteless after a few days. So, too, was Loreto's attitude towards Mario, whose promise to come down from his second-class accommodations to check on the girls every day was broken. As the trip progressed, he would come down less and less often. There was no worse time for him to decide to do this than when, just a few days into their trip, rumors began to spread that there were German submarines nearby.

For several days after that rumor began to spread, people were on edge, thinking that at any moment, the ship could be targeted. While they weren't aboard a warship, German submarines were known for striking innocent ships to send a message or assert their dominance. Loreto remembered her mother telling her stories about the Germans before her father left for America again—when it seemed all too real that a draft could occur and he could be shipped off to war.

There were lighter days to follow, where morale was a bit higher. And there was no higher point with regard to joy than when whales decided to swim alongside the ship for a day. Once Loreto had heard about this, she didn't hesitate. She grabbed her sisters and headed to the back of the ship.

Once they were able to squeeze their way out onto the observation deck to see, it was a magnificent sight. One that Loreto and Lena would never forget, and they had both hoped Carolina wouldn't forget either. Large whales nearly a quarter of the size of the ship swam alongside, backs up against the surface of the water. None of the girls had ever seen a whale before and the sight of it alone was exhilarating. But what *really* got them was when the whales would shoot water up and out of what some passengers around them were calling blowholes. That got the girls laughing wildly, and Loreto had no choice but to join in.

The whales hung around for a long time, and the waves they created started to make a lot of the passengers sick. By this point, the girls were all in the women's quarters and lying in their beds, talking about their father and how they would tell him all about the whales. They wondered, too, if he had seen any on his journeys across the ocean.

The next few days were uneventful. No whales. No seasick passengers. And, of course, no change in meal planning. Loreto was ready to get on dry land and eat solid food again. There was also no sign of Mario for several days. The trip had been more than halfway over and the girls were seeing less and less of him. Loreto had no idea how much her father had to pay the man to look out for them, but whatever it was, he wasn't living up to it.

After sixteen days on the water, the girls had finally made it to the shores of America. On a beautiful, September day, they sailed into the New York Harbor and felt the joy their father had mentioned in letters sent back home. He wrote about people crying with happiness, hugging, cheering, celebrating. Little American flags seemed to appear out of nowhere. Everyone on the ship was coming here to create a new life, and this would be day one of their journey.

Amid the excitement, Mario made his way down into steerage and to the girls. He had a big smile sitting beneath his mustache and waved to them as if they would be excited to see him. Loreto refused to return the greeting. She simply stared at the man, intently, and that seemed to wipe the smile from his face. He could feel the hostility and Loreto knew it. *Good*, she thought to herself. The man deserved it.

He waved and told the girls to follow him. They did, and he led them to the back of the ship and out to the observation deck. It was crowded. Shoulder to shoulder. There was seemingly no way to be able to see anything. Mario wiggled his way through the crowd and the girls followed. And once he hit his farthest point, he bent down, picked up Carolina, and put her on his shoulders so she could see. Then he pointed in the direction where all eyes were focused.

That's when Loreto saw it: The Statue of Liberty.

CHAPTER 22

The ship stood still, docked in Manhattan while the first- and second-class passengers received their examination by doctors above deck. The steerage passengers remained in their place, waiting for the final transport to Ellis Island where they would be examined.

Mario, finally earning his money, remained with them. Loreto had grown tired of the man and his lack of oversight during the trip. She thought it was selfish of him to leave three girls to fend for themselves in the steerage compartment of the ship for 16 days.

But the trip was now over. And as she and her sisters stepped off the ship with Mario, she thought to herself that soon she would be with her family in Cleveland.

Her father had written letters home preparing

them for the journey. He had mentioned the potential for rough seas, which, luckily, only occurred on the day the whales swam with the ship. What he also mentioned in his letters was the thrill they would all feel when they would first see The Statue of Liberty, which they did. And the grandness of Great Hall, where they would be examined by doctors before entering the country. In his written words, he walked them through the process of being assigned numbers, put into groups, and sent off to their destinations. He also told them about The Kissing Post on Ellis Island, where family members already in America would first be able to see their emigrant family members. Unfortunately, Vico had let his girls know that he wouldn't be able to make it there to greet them. The toll of paying for their trip would leave him with nothing, so he couldn't afford to get there, nor could he afford to skip work.

Once they entered the building, they followed the crowd up a winding, long staircase and then Mario was separated from them and sent into a line designated for men. As they entered Great Hall, Loreto thought back to the words her father had used to describe the place.

Giant.

Magnificent.

Crowded.

It was certainly all three. But the tall ceilings were what stuck out to her the most. They seemed to go on forever, and Loreto caught herself staring up at the ceiling for too long, nervous when she looked back down that her sisters would be lost in the crowd of people.

They weren't. Loreto and the girls remained in the line for women. It was a slow-moving line that ended with a physical exam from a doctor. As they waited, doctors walked up and down the line and briefly looked at people. Loreto knew they were looking for obvious signs of sickness and disease in order to prevent people from entering the new country with preexisting conditions. It was necessary, sure, but it felt uncomfortable having people walk past them so often, looking for signs of something.

Loreto knew the chances of being denied were low. Her father had told her about how few people he saw—and heard about through talks with others in Cleveland—that were denied entry. And she would find out later in life that there were only about two percent of people denied entry to America due to physical or mental incapacity. Still, the feeling was nerve-racking. And would become even more so.

As they made their way to the front of the line, Loreto watched as some women were taken away and given marks either on their forehead or their shoulder. Some would have an X written on their shoulder, yet some had white letters written on their head. One woman looked to be hiding a pregnancy and was taken away with *PG* written on her head, two letters she recognized from her native language. It was a chaotic time for sure, and then the girls finally made their way to the front of the line where they were examined by a doctor. Loreto went first and then helped to control Carolina while she was examined. No marks were put on either girl and few words were spoken from the doctor to the interpreter by his side, but all smiles seemed to indicate good things.

And then Lena went for her examination. The doctor began to examine her but slowed and began looking intently into her eyes. His smile was gone— not like it was when he was examining Carolina and Loreto. After a short stare into her, he leaned back and drew a piece of chalk from his waist. He placed one hand on Lena's head and then the action he did seemed to occur in slow motion. It was something that they had seen happen to so few people in the line. But when it did, the reactions were traumatic. Desperate. Pleading.

With his other hand, the doctor drew a letter on Lena's forehead. He drew an E. Then he waved for a colleague of his to come over and just as quickly as Loreto and Carolina had been approved to enter the country, Lena was denied.

CHAPTER 23

*L*oreto was frantic. Lena was pulled out of line, and she had to pick up Carolina and follow the man who was escorting her somewhere else. She kept yelling to the man, asking him why the doctor had placed a white mark on her forehead.

Perchè lo hai fatto? Why did you do it?

She continued to scream it, but the noise echoing through Great Hall was so loud that her cries were muffled. Why did he do that? What had he seen in Lena that made him mark her as unable to enter the country? What would happen now?

She followed and they were taken to another room, still grand in size but with far less people. And the people who were in this room had all been marked like Lena had. There were white chalk marks on nearly every person's forehead, and others had a simple X on their shoulder, or an X with a circle drawn around it. She would learn later that the X on someone's shoulder stood for the possibility of mental incapacitation while the X with a circle around it meant the possibility had turned to a confirmation. And the letters written in white chalk on the foreheads of emigrants stood for which possible condition needed to be checked. For Lena, the E on her forehead meant she had a potential problem with her eyes that needed further examination.

The room where they sat and waited had wooden benches in the middle but very few people were sitting. They were too anxious to learn their fate. For Loreto, she had no idea what she would do if Lena was turned away. No idea how she would go back home. How she would notify her dad. Or how she would notify Mario for that matter. Since he had been placed into the line for men, they had been separated. And given his actions while onboard the ship, she didn't doubt the idea that they would never see him again.

It took an examination with an eye doctor to discover that Lena did not have trachoma, which the initial doctor thought she may have had. The disease is one that can cause blindness and death and when Loreto discovered this, she found more relief in her sister's health than in their being able to enter America.

She was ready to get out of there. Great Hall was a wonderful sight as they exited the ship and went into the place that was supposed to be the first, exciting leg of their journey on American soil, but it was turning out to be a headache. Scary. Unfamiliar territory that Loreto, a sixteen-year-old girl thrown into this role of a mother on the morning they left for this move, was finding to be difficult. And stressful. She just wanted to get to her father and have this whole process come to an end.

They weren't done with the examinations yet, though. There would be one more psychological evaluation that they would have to go through. And this included Lena and Carolina, although they were both young children. The process was short, only taking about two minutes of questions regarding ideals and views on America, but would need to be done by all three girls.

When they were done—and passed—they were led outside and to the other end of the island where there were many people hugging, crying, and kissing. This, Loreto knew when she saw it, was The Kissing Post her father had told her about in letters. The people kissing and hugging and crying tears of joy were the family members greeting emigrants for the first time in America. The excitement of their new life was in full bloom. Making it to The Kissing Post meant you had passed all of your tests and were granted entrance into the country.

The Kissing Post is where the girls would catch their ferry to Manhattan where they could use the money sent by their father to buy train tickets from New York to Cleveland. That was the only thing separating them from their dad. And that thought alone made Loreto want to cry right along with the others at the famous post.

She thought about how close they had come to being sent home. Or separated. She and her mother had heard horror stories over the years on the Italian countryside of families being torn apart by the examination process. How a family with several children would make the journey to America only to have one child turned away for a medical condition and the rest granted entry. The family would then have to determine which parent would go back to their home country with their denied child and which would stay with the children granted access. Taking the entire family home simply wasn't an option. America had opportunities that were far too great to pass up, and if families had to split up that was what they did.

Loreto realized how close they were to having that dilemma occur. Lena would have to be sent home which meant they would make the decision that they would all go home. Loreto wouldn't be able to send an eight-year-old on a ship across the Atlantic by herself. They would all go. Go back onto that ship. Back across the Atlantic for sixteen days. In rough seas, eating soup and bread. Back home to their sick mother.

The tears poured down her cheeks as she realized just how lucky they had been. They were now standing in a large crowd of people, waiting for their ferry to take them across the harbor and into the city. Mario was nowhere to be found and none of the girls spoke any English. Things would certainly be difficult from here, but they were at least going to be in the country.

They were Americans.

CHAPTER 24

They were placed on a double-decker ferry and carried along the harbor with the rest of the newest Americans. There wasn't a sad face on the boat. It was full of cheer. Of different languages all floating around, and Loreto would grow excited when she could hear others speaking Italian. She wondered if they would be headed towards Cleveland, too, where her father had said so many Italians were living.

To this point, everything her father had written had been accurate with regard to what they should expect once they hit Ellis Island. The marking on Lena's forehead was an unexpected event, but the rest was correct. This turned out to be true for the money exchange and the purchase of train tickets for the girls as well. And then they made their way into Manhattan where the site of a major city with tall, brick buildings several stories high was an awe-striking moment for all the girls.

They walked through the streets—three girls without the supervision of Mario, who was now considered by Loreto to be a lost cause—in amazement. They were in America. Americans. This was the dream their father had since the moment Loreto was born sixteen years before. The only person they were missing was their mother, and Loreto couldn't wait to get to Cleveland so she could write to her that she and the girls were safe. Happy. Excited to see *her* once Dr. Portofino would say it was safe for her to travel.

Without the help of Mario, transporting the bags was the duty of Loreto, and Lena carried Carolina when she couldn't walk. She was happy to find that the train station wasn't too far from where the ferry had dropped them off. Once they arrived, they boarded a train headed to Cleveland, and she found a spot for them to sit together. The ride to Cleveland would be fifteen hours long and she wanted to make sure that the girls—Carolina especially—could get some sleep.

As the train departed from New York, the girls grew more excited. The next stop on their trip would be in Cleveland. It had been a long few weeks of traveling, and they were ready to rest in one place where they would have one of their parents again. Loreto thought she had done a pretty good job at keeping the girls safe but was ready to have the help of her father.

The train drifted through New York City and the girls sat quietly, looking out the window at a land that looked so different from home. Everything was flat. There were no hills, but there were lots of buildings. America didn't start to look similar to the Italian countryside until they reached central Pennsylvania on their way west. By this point, Carolina and Lena were both asleep. Carolina was sprawled across the seat with her head on Loreto's lap and Lena was sitting on the other side, resting on her shoulder. She took comfort in knowing she was awake to protect them. If this trip had taught her anything, it was that she would one day be a great mother. A good caretaker to her children. She felt as though this trip would be much harsher than anything she might endure as a mother and homemaker living under one roof and sleeping in the same bed every night.

The girls had woken by the time the train traveled through the city of Pittsburgh on its way to Cleveland. This was one of the final stops before they were set to get off and as each stop occurred, the girls would watch as train passengers would step off and be greeted with open arms by waiting family members. Tears would flow just like they had at The Kissing Post on Ellis Island. And after a short while, those smiling, hugging families would float away as the train carried on with its route. Pittsburgh was the last one before the stop would be made in Cleveland.

Loreto wondered if her father was there already. He knew that today was the day they were set to make it to their new home city, but he wouldn't know what time unless asking at the train station. Maybe he had, or maybe he needed to work. She hoped for the former. She wanted him to be there. She wanted the hugs and kisses she had seen others receive along the way and wanted to have that embrace by her father.

She looked at her sisters when the train was out of Pittsburgh and said, "Penso che saremo i prossimi." *I think we're next.* And they all shared an excited smile. This was confirmed just a few short minutes later when the train conductor said something in English. They didn't understand any of what he said, except for the last word: *Cleveland.*

They stared intently. Looked out the window. Tried to look toward the front of the train to see when green pastures would turn into homes and streets—that's how they would know Cleveland was close. It seemed to take days, but it was only a few hours. Lena was the first to notice something ahead and shouted loud enough for the entire train to hear: "Guarda!" *Look!*

Others sleeping in the same train car didn't appreciate the shout and some gave stares over their way, but the girls didn't care. Loreto smiled at the people giving begrudging looks and shared in on her sister's excitement. Their three faces remained pressed against the window as they watched the city slowly zoom into view. Eventually, it appeared. The train rolled past rows of homes set up much like the old streets of Termoli, where Loreto would visit her grandparents. Everything was condensed. Close together. Much unlike the farm they had lived on for so long.

The train whistled and began to slow, and Loreto's heart was in her throat. She wanted to laugh, wanted to cry, wanted to scream all at once.

The conductor hollered out something else that none of the girls could understand, but it sounded like some numbers. A sign along the tracks read some English words and the number 110 next to it— what she would soon learn was the 110th Street train station in Cleveland.

Skies were cloudy and the weather was lousy on that afternoon, but spirits were bright. The girls looked out the window and when the train came to a slow roll in front of the station, the other side of the window had nothing but smiling faces beneath hats and scarves. Black jackets were draped over the shoulders of many onlookers and all the attire made it tough to spot whether or not their father was there. It had been more than a year since they had seen him last and his look could have changed, as it had when he left the first time. Loreto couldn't remember much from his first return home, but she did remember how her mother had mentioned several times how he had looked older. The same may have taken place this time around.

The train stopped. A loud whistle went off. The doors opened and people began to pour out. Loreto had to grab the bags and she didn't want Lena to carry Carolina through the crowd, so they waited a few minutes until the storm of people died down. Then she grabbed the bags and Lena grabbed Carolina. They walked down the steps and onto the platform of the train station, entering Cleveland for the first time. There were people everywhere, and it was hard to spot anyone. Loreto was the tallest of the three and tried peeking above and between people standing, chatting with their loved ones. She tried to shout *Papa!* a few times, but so many heads turned— there were so many Papas in the crowd. They looked. They walked. And then they finally heard his voice.

"Le mie ragazze!" *My girls!*

Loreto turned toward the sound and saw her father running toward them. He removed his hat from his head, dropped to one knee, opened his arms and took all his girls in at once. Loreto dropped her bags and embraced her father like she had done as a six-year-old when he came back home from his first trip to America. The family held each other for several minutes. Their father kissed the foreheads of each of his daughters and continued to pull them in tight.

The embrace was welcomed. For the past few weeks, Loreto had to do all of the embracing. The protecting. The nurturing. And it was nice to be the one being held again. She enjoyed each second of it.

Her father pulled back and then looked around before asking, "Dov'è Mario?"

The girls looked at Loreto and she looked at her father and shrugged. She told him about the journey to the ship and how he was helpful, but once on the ship he became less and less reliable. And then she told him about being separated from him at Ellis Island and not seeing him again after that.

Vico's eyes grew wide with rage, and Loreto wished she hadn't said anything. Or that he hadn't asked. She wanted to embrace the happiness of this moment for as long as she could. And he must have seen that disappointment in her eyes because his anger dissipated. He took it back and brought the smile out again. That was when two people walked up behind him and smiled down at the girls.

Vico turned around to see them and then stood. He introduced the two to his daughters. They were Aunt Tomasina and Uncle Francisco, who everyone here called Uncle Charlie. They had been in America for more than a decade but still spoke Italian, which was a relief to Loreto. Lena and Carolina may not have been expecting anything otherwise, but Loreto knew they would all be staying with Uncle Charlie and Aunt Tomasina and worried that they would quickly need to adapt to the English language. She was happy to find that this wasn't the case.

Vico grabbed his daughter's bags in one hand and still managed to pick up Carolina with the other. *Come on*, he said in Italian. *Let's go show you where we'll be staying.*

Aunt Tomasina walked between Lena and Loreto and placed each of her hands in one of theirs. She was a sweet woman with a soft voice and she paid special attention to Loreto, asking her questions about the journey and congratulating her on being such a reliable young woman. She repeatedly told her how amazing she would be as a mother—something Loreto thought to herself recently and felt comfort in hearing from someone else.

They walked to an electric car stop where Aunt Tomasina said they would get a ride to their home on 125th Street. When it arrived, Lena agonized at the thought of another train ride, which sent a giggle through Aunt Tomasina and Uncle Charlie, who both assured her it was a quick trip and nothing like the train.

Loreto, though, was paying attention to her father, who didn't react to the comment. His mind was elsewhere, and she knew where. She saw that rage in his eyes when she mentioned that Mario had left them, and although he didn't allow it to ruin his initial moment with his daughters, he wasn't about to let it go. His eyes were wide. He was off, somewhere else, *thinking about* something else. Loreto was worried that what she had said would cause her father to go after Mario.

PART IV
THE TRAGEDY

*V*ico couldn't believe it. Mario charged him $100 and for what? He did nothing. He took the money and allowed himself a journey to the home country and back on Vico's dime. When the girls stepped off the train in Cleveland, they struggled to carry their own bags. Mario was nowhere in sight. Rage grew inside Vico and the only thing that pulled him from his thoughts of retaliation was Loreto's voice: "Papa?"

When he looked over, he noticed that the train car had stopped. Charlie, Tomasina, and his daughters had all stepped off, down onto the street, and were waiting for him.

"Spiacente." *Sorry*.

Vico stepped down onto 125th Street carrying the bags of his daughters. As the train car departed behind him, he allowed his bitter thoughts of Mario to ride with it. He hadn't seen his daughters in so long and now they were here, right in front of him, and he didn't want to allow Mario's actions to spoil the moment. He smiled, nodded his head, and said *Let's go show you to your new home.*

The group made their way down 125th Street and onto Catawba Street where Uncle Charlie and Aunt Tomasina's house sat. When they reached the door, they were greeted by the smiles of five children varying in age. Loreto, Lena, and Carolina were introduced to their cousins. Anthony, the oldest, was born in Italy and was five years old when Uncle Charlie and Aunt Tomasina made the move across the Atlantic. The others—Maria, Carmella, Jimmy, and Louise—were all born in America. Vico watched as his girls embraced their cousins for the first time and then were given a tour of the house. Eight kids and three adults certainly made the place seem a bit more cramped than Vico was used to when he would come over for dinner, but the smiles on Charlie and Tomasina's faces didn't show similar discomfort.

As his girls were shown to where they would sleep, Vico put down their bags and thanked his uncle and aunt again for their hospitality. No longer living in Mrs. Carlluci's home would allow him to save until he was able to buy himself and the girls their own home. He let his aunt and uncle know this again and again, trying to provide them comfort with the situation.

Aunt Tomasina and Uncle Charlie had been incredibly helpful during both occasions Vico was in America and continued to say they had no problems with the arrangement. The only thing they required of him was to purchase four more chairs to place around the kitchen table, which he did. It was a tight squeeze to fit all eleven people around one table, but they made do.

LORETO HAD NEVER SEEN a home with two levels in it before. Walking up a set of stairs inside of a home was new to her. Back in Mirabella, everything inside their house was on one level. There were steps on the sides of some steep hills in town, but other than that, stairs inside of a home weren't something she was accustomed to.

As she and her sisters were shown around by their cousins, there was a certain level of excitement mixed with timidness. For Loreto and Anthony, most of the conversation was quieter, more mature. The younger kids though, especially Carolina, were simply excited at the new living arrangements. She was excited to be in a new environment. And also happy to be done with the long travels.

Aunt Tomasina made her way upstairs after a while and coordinated sleeping arrangements. She also asked the girls if they were hungry and thirsty, turning to Loreto last and asking her in a much different tone. While she spoke to Lena and Carolina with the enthusiasm one would use when speaking to a child, Aunt Tomasina gave Loreto the respect a young woman who had just traveled to a new continent with her two younger sisters would deserve. She spoke to Loreto as if she was speaking to another grown woman, and she gave a smile while doing so that showed just how courageous she thought Loreto was, and Loreto was happy to see that. She had gone through so much over the past few weeks and felt happy knowing that even though times were rough at moments, she was able to safely bring her sisters to their final destination.

Once nighttime came and the group was ready to have their first dinner under the same roof, there wasn't a single frown. As chairs were organized around the table and bodies circled, looking for where to best place themselves, new cousins were trying to sit beside each other and the adults were simply looking to settle down the energetic little ones and get situated. Aunt Tomasina had made plenty of food and Vico had thanked her several times, making Lena, Carolina, and Loreto follow suit.

The good-natured attitudes toward one another would soon fade, though. Vico continued to work long days and save his money to move the family into their own house, but it wasn't fast enough. The added expense of a family of four living inside their home caused Uncle Charlie and Aunt Tomasina to begin quickly changing their attitude toward the situation. Loreto could feel the resentment slowly growing, and although it wasn't towards the girls directly, it was their presence that made the situation worse. While Vico was gone, the girls would remain in the home, and the stress began to grow on Aunt Tomasina in particular.

> *September 1915*
> *Dear Carmina,*
> *As I write this letter I hope and pray you*
> *   are feeling better. The girls are*
> *   wonderful and I am so happy to have*
> *   them here. I know you must miss them*
> *   dearly but I know we will soon all be*
> *   together. We are somewhat crowded here*
> *   between our family and Uncle Charlies.*
> *   The sooner we can be on our own the*
> *   better it will be. I continue to miss you*
> *   with all my heart. I will write again in a*
> *   short time.*
> *Love, Vico*

Although Loreto tried her hardest to help her

aunt, there seemed to be nothing she could do to relieve the situation. On most nights, she would lie in her bed and yearn for her mother. But she had no idea what her mother was going through. Soon, though, she would find out.

CHAPTER 26

*U*ncle Charlie walked in the house one day after work and Loreto could see a look of concern on his face. He called his wife into the other room, and Loreto watched as they looked at a letter —something that had come in the mail and had concerned them both. Aunt Tomasina had covered her mouth and shook her head and while Loreto wanted to rush into the other room and snatch the letter, she knew better than to pry into her aunt and uncle's mail pile.

Somehow, though, she knew what was in that letter. She knew it had something to do with her mother.

Their cousins tried to entertain as much as they could and for the most part, they did a good job. There were ice cream socials and potluck dinners held at the local church, and neighborhood picnics where families would come together to talk and get to know one another. The girls were getting to know other families in the area and enjoyed making friends. One of the families they encountered most often was a nice, middle-aged couple: the Santangelos. Loreto had learned from her Aunt Tomasina that the Santangelos were unable to have their own children and were therefore happy to be around any kids they could. Mr. Santangelo often spent his time playing games with the children during get-togethers, and Mrs. Santangelo would help to prepare meals and desserts for them. They were a truly genuine couple, but Loreto noticed their exceptional liking of Carolina. She was the perfect age—an energetic toddler who could make any adult laugh with her carelessness.

The Santangelos would also frequently stop by and visit as a friendly gesture, knowing Aunt Tomasina could use a breather from all of the kids. One evening while they were there, Loreto heard her father come through the door after a long day of work. He would come home late, and filthy. He was always hungry, tired, and she could overhear him making promises to his aunt and uncle that he and the girls would be able to move out soon.

He kept working hard—so hard that his girls were barely able to see him. They would be happy to see him as he walked through the door, but on the night he came home after the curious letter came in the mail, Loreto didn't allow her sisters to grab onto his legs first. She stormed up to him and asked him to confront Aunt Tomasina and Uncle Charlie to ask them what the letter was about. His eyelids were heavy and he looked worn, but he nodded none-theless as he, too, was curious about his wife's condi-tion and when she would be able to come to America. The family needed her.

Loreto stayed behind as she watched her father approach his aunt and uncle in the other room. Uncle Charlie was reading his newspaper and Aunt Tomasina had taken to her sewing, which she did often as a form of relief from tending to the house and kids. As her father approached the two, she could see them stop what they were doing and look at each other, then Uncle Charlie gave his wife a nod and stood. Loreto wasn't able to hear what they were saying, but when Uncle Charlie bent down and picked up a letter from the table beside him, she knew exactly what it was and she walked over to her father without hesitation.

As a sixteen-year-old, she didn't need to act as though she was fearful of reprimand. She was a young woman and one who had every right to know if that letter had information regarding her mother's whereabouts.

"Papa," she called to her father as she approached.

As he turned, she could see the letter in his hand and he reached out and put an arm around her. He told her it was from Gilda Brunetti, their friend from home who promised she would look after their mother. The two of them read the handwriting together and at the end, Vico held Loreto as she cried. She so desperately wanted her mother to be here with them, and then this letter came and seemed to shatter all hope.

Trying to make her feel better, she heard her father's words in her ear telling her that *Everything will be okay. She will be here soon. I'll make sure of it.* But there was no way he could do that and she knew it.

As her father headed off to get cleaned up from work, she wondered whether or not she should let her sisters know what was contained within the note from Gilda. Lena would only get upset and Carolina may not even comprehend. She thought to herself that it might be better to keep quiet. Maybe they would ask in a few days or weeks and then she could tell them. Otherwise, she wanted to allow them to keep the joy in the hearts that they had when playing with their cousins or other kids on the street.

Instead of saying anything to her sisters, she got caught up in watching them. From the doorway to the bedroom shared by her youngest cousins, she watched the kids playing and talking. She saw the smiles on the faces of her sisters and thought back to their time back home in Italy. Being in America had treated them well, but she consistently fantasized about being back home, in Mirabella, on the farm. It was where she felt most safe. And most herself. Here, in America, houses connected to each other and there were always people walking around. It was so unlike the openness of her hometown and while it was exciting at first, she was ready for a break from it.

She was happy to see her sisters smiling, though. They had much more to keep them entertained here than they did back home. Carolina, for sure, was loving the constant levels of energy around her. And if Loreto was to admit it, she was getting a break from having to do all the entertaining the way she did back home.

Her thoughts were thrown when she felt a hand on her shoulder. It was her father, now cleaned and in dry clothes. With his hand still on her shoulder, he looked to his two other girls playing and asked Loreto if she had told them. "No," she said. "Dovrei?" *Should I?*

"Sì," her father said, and then he walked into the room to get his two girls. They all went to the kitchen table and sat to talk. With only the four of them, the table seemed giant. So unlike the cramped space it was during dinnertime. Loreto sat on one side of the table with Carolina and Lena sat with Vico across from them. He held up the note for his daughters to see, then nodded to Loreto to let her know she could tell them of its contents.

Mom is ill, she told her younger sisters. *Very ill.*

And she won't be able to make it to be here with us anytime soon. As expected, Lena began to cry for her mother, but Carolina didn't quite comprehend. She looked at Lena as she cried and then up at Loreto with wide eyes as if to ask why Lena was upset. Loreto, knowing she didn't understand the magnitude of what was happening, simply grabbed her and pulled her in close. On the other side of the table, Vico embraced his middle daughter as she cried.

Loreto wondered about some of the things Gilda mentioned in the letter. About how her mother's heart seemed to be failing and how depression could be the cause. And how Dr. Portofino had begun to see this is a more common issue with families whose travel to America caused long periods of separation. Gilda wrote in her letter that time would be the only way to heal their mother's heart condition and that she would need to get better medically before she would be able to withstand the long journey to be with her family.

Something in her thought otherwise and at that very moment, she began to cry just as hard as Lena was on the other side of the table. She buried her face into innocent little Carolina's head and she cried.

CHAPTER 27

*V*ico had lost enthusiasm for clocking out at the end of a hard day of work at Asher Metalworks. It had been nearly a month since his daughters had come to be with him in America, and he was worried he had sent for them prematurely. The extra money he paid Mario Giuliani to oversee their trip certainly put a dent in the money he had saved, but he thought it to be a good investment at the time.

Now? Not so much.

He worried about Carmina back home and whether or not she was getting better. He wondered about his daughters and how they were feeling about their living conditions, especially since he was almost always gone, working. And he also worried about Uncle Charlie and Aunt Tomasina who had been nothing short of amazing with the entire situation but, he could sense, were starting to lose their patience. They wanted their house back to themselves.

Vico walked the streets on his way back home like he did every night at dusk. As the sun set behind the rowhomes that lined the city streets, he found himself walking past Grotto Bar. He hadn't stepped foot in the place since his indiscretion with the bartender, Julia Torolli. As he could every night when he walked by, he heard the sounds coming from inside the bar. He heard people playing music and also some shouting. It came muffled through the door as it always had, yet today, unlike any day since he and Julia had their night together, he was tempted to walk in and relax for a bit. Going from a stressful situation at work to an even more stressful situation at home was weighing on him. He knew he shouldn't spend the money on a beer or two when he was desperately trying to save everything to get himself and his girls into their own place, but the idea sounded so relaxing. So therapeutic. The idea of simply sitting on a chair and enjoying a drink in peace was enticing. So much so that he caved to that idea.

When he pulled on the handle of the bar door, stale air poured out and the scene had hit him all over again. When he had come here before, he never allowed himself to overindulge—mostly because he was saving for his family to come over—but not everyone else was the same. There were some men who had sat inside this bar from the time they quit work until the time the lights shut off inside. They were the ones who blew through everything they had, and all these weeks later Vico still recognized some of the faces. The workday had barely ended and already there were droopy eyelids and loud voices.

Back when he and Julia spoke a lot, he remembered her mentioning which day of the week she had off from work. He couldn't remember which day it was but he hoped it was this day. He didn't want to see her. Wasn't entirely sure he would know what to say if he did. He just wanted a beer and to sit and think for a while.

As he walked past the tables and toward a vacant barstool that sat before a wooden bar top, he looked around for her. His eyes traveled across a sea of loud men sitting at tables with half-full pitchers and individual mugs in front of them. They laughed, they talked, they shouted, and none of them seemed to realize that the world was going on around them. There was no empathizing over whether or not the other patrons wanted to hear their obscenities.

As he continued toward the bar, he felt more and more relief when there was no sign of Julia. She wasn't serving any table, wasn't behind the bar, wasn't seemingly anywhere. But in his search, he came across another familiar face. One he *truly* didn't want to see. One that altered his mood in an instant, bringing him from exhausted and calm to energetic and fuming with rage. The pudgy little man with the tiny nose that he recognized was none other than Mario Giuiliani, the son of a bitch who took Vico's one-hundred-dollar payment to help his girls get across the Atlantic, only to leave them high and dry when they needed him most.

Vico continued toward the bar, talking himself out of his rage in the process. *Leave it alone*, he told himself. *Nothing good will come of a confrontation*. And when he reached that empty barstool he had his eye on, he told himself he was calm.

Behind the bar was a man he didn't recognize, cleaning the mugs and placing them into a rack. The burly owner of the bar, Tony Musso, was sitting in a chair behind the bar, glasses hanging low on his face and sheets of paper in front of him. But, again, there was no sign of Julia. A part of him felt relief but another part was upset about the fact. He might have told himself he didn't want to see her, but he really did. She showed him love and compassion, and it had been so long since he'd had someone express those feelings to him. Even for just a friendly conversation, he thought to himself that he would have liked to see her.

The man washing the mugs saw Vico take a seat and then said something in English that he didn't understand. He was accustomed to hearing some English throughout the foundry during his work days, but for the most part everyone still spoke Italian. He had no idea what the man said but gauging his body language, he wasn't ready to be serving a beer just yet. So Vico waited, uncomfortably, wondering if he should shout his order for a mug of beer or wait for another sign from the man.

He waited. And the man continued drying mugs. Then he shouted something into the back of the bar and although he spoke in English, there was one term that he recognized. It was a name. A familiar one.

Then she walked out. It was Julia. And he felt his eyes widen at her sight before he quickly told himself not to show so much expression on his face. After all, he had spent a night with this girl and then never spoke to her. For all he knew, she might have been furious with him.

As she walked out from behind the bar, she began to speak to the man cleaning the mugs. Her eyes had yet to meet Vico's, and he told himself to be prepared for the worst. To be prepared for anger or sadness on her part. But when the bartender pointed over at him and she looked, she gave him nothing but a wide-eyed smile. "Vico!" she yelled as she walked over. "How are you?"

He shrugged his shoulders.

She poured him a drink and stood before him. In her native tongue, she said, "Sorry. Speaking English has become a force of habit. Tony is having us learn English." Then she asked him how he'd been, what he'd been up to, and how it was going with his daughters. She mentioned nothing of their night together, nor did she show a sign of being upset. This troubled Vico because he thought to himself that he must not have mattered much to her. Or maybe what she did was common with the patrons of the bar, and he was simply Julia's flavor of the week.

He caught her up on what was going on and then, fearfully, asked her how things had been going at the bar and in her life. Her answer was about as basic as it can get and then, at the request of some slurring men at the other end of the bar, she had to walk away. This left him to ponder everything between the two of them. First, wondering if it was all worth it to hurt his wife. What if word got back about it? What if that was the reason for her depression? Or was she not depressed at all, but simply delayed coming to America because she didn't want to see him?

A million and one thoughts popped into his head, and he took a few long sips of the drink in front of him to try to clear those thoughts. He wanted Julia to come back and talk to him some more so he could be distracted. Distracted from his life, distracted from his problems, and distracted from the voice in the corner growing louder and louder as time went on.

He peered over his shoulder at the man from time to time but would find the restraint to turn around and ignore the man. Tried to, at least. But it was difficult. After peeking over his shoulder about a dozen times, he finally swung his entire body around in his stool. With his back now pressed against the bar, he simply observed the man he had such a hatred for. And when he could take it no longer, he took one long swig of his beer, slammed his mug down on the bar, and did what he wanted to do since he laid eyes on the man.

"Hey!" Vico shouted at Mario in Italian. "You've got some sort of nerve leaving my girls in New York City. I paid you!"

Mario looked up and right at Vico with no surprise on his face, as if he'd already seen him walk in and prepared himself for the possibility of an altercation. "I did as you asked," he said, holding out his palms.

That nonchalant, bullshit answer only sent Vico spiraling into a deeper rage. All that time, all those images of confronting Mario, and not one of the imagined scenarios had him showing such little remorse.

Vico suddenly stood and made his way over to Mario without breaking his stride. Mario looked up at Vico with a grin on his face that said *Oh, come on. What are you going to do?*

Vico did exactly what he wanted to do. He pulled his arm back and punched Mario in the mouth. Mario fell back out of his chair and went to the floor, and Vico didn't stop. He leaned over and was able to get three more good punches in before Mario's bar buddies ripped him off and pushed him back. Some other patrons jumped in and grabbed Vico while Mario's friends picked him up from the ground.

To his side, Vico saw Julia, both of her arms holding his. He shrugged her off, as well as the others that were holding him. He rearranged his clothes and situated himself. The entire bar watched Mario get brought to his feet, wipe his mouth and see the blood coming from it. Vico could see a flare in Mario's eyes when he saw the blood, but he wasn't concerned. He got what he deserved, and Vico got the relief he felt *he* deserved.

I'll kill you, Vico! That was the last thing Vico remembered the man saying.

CHAPTER 28

$\mathcal{I}$t took only a matter of moments before the patrons of the bar were back to their seats, doing their thing as if nothing had happened. As if Mario hadn't been punched repeatedly by Vico before being saved by his friends.

Julia walked Vico back to his seat, asking him in the process what the hell that was all about. She made her way around to the back of the bar, poured him another mug of beer, and then listened as he told her the story of Mario's deception—how he took Vico's money yet used it as an excursion for himself rather than a work assignment. And then he started telling her about his wife. And how she was sick and couldn't come with the girls and how she was, as it seemed now, in worsening condition and unable to come for a while.

Julia knew he had a wife before they had gotten

together, but he felt the need to tell her the story because he wanted to reiterate. He wanted to let her know how much he loved Carmina and that he needed her here to be with him. He was trying to get a point across to her that what they did was wrong and wasn't going to happen again. Julia, being a smart girl, knew exactly what he was trying to say.

"I hope she can be here with you soon," she said to him. "I'd like you to be happy."

In all the time they spent together, Julia was never a confrontational person. Even when he sat there and admitted to her that he felt guilty about sleeping with her, she remained upbeat and positive. He let her know this and told her that when she *did* find someone who she could be with, she would make an amazing wife.

Her response to this wasn't what he imagined. "I think I'll just keep having fun," she said with a sly smile.

And there it was. One of the questions he had asked himself was whether or not she cared for him or whether she cared for many of the men who visited this bar. It seemed the latter was the answer. And as she walked away to tend to some empty mugs throughout the place, he could only look at her and smile. It was a smile of relief. He knew that he and Carmina loved each other and that his night with Julia was a fluke. Not only that, but there would be no issues when Carmina came here. Julia wouldn't be wondering whether Vico would be choosing her over his wife. There would be no domestic issues. No disputes. No arguing. Julia was simply having fun while she was young and beautiful. And those two things she certainly was.

Vico finished his beer and left his change on the bar. He grabbed his coat and his lunchbox from his workday and headed for the door. He took one last look back at Julia who was now in conversation with a table of three men, all smiling, all hoping they'll be the lucky one to end up capturing her attention.

He was happy for her and as the door closed behind him and he stepped out into the crisp, night air, he felt like he was closing the door on one of the few mistakes he'd made in his life. He was ready to have Carmina by his side again. The two of them had sacrificed so much of their own lives to make a better future for their daughters in a new country and he was ready to have her back. As he strode through the empty streets of Cleveland and back to Uncle Charlie and Aunt Tomasina's house, he tried to calculate how much money he had and what he would need in order to get his own place, bring the girls, and send word for Carmina to join them when she was ready. And he knew she would be ready soon. He was sure of it. And excited for the day it would finally happen.

Vico had only made it a block or so away from Grotto Bar when a shadowy figure stepped out from an alley and into the yellow light that shone from the street lamp a few feet above the figure's head. The figure wore a black coat and a short-brimmed hat, and when it lifted its head, Vico saw the recognizable face.

"Go home, Mario," he said in their native language, and then he started walking again. The store windows along the street were all dark. Businesses were closed and it was nighttime for many families. It seemed the only life in all of Cleveland at the moment was in Mario and Vico.

Mario stepped out further into the street as Vico went to walk by, which stopped Vico in his tracks again. Now, standing only a few feet apart, Vico spoke once more: "Go home, Mario."

"No."

"No?"

"Not until you apologize."

That's when the silver revolver became visible. And within an instant, Vico's entire mentality had changed. The events that took place afterward happened so quickly that Vico hardly had time to think. And before he knew it, he was lying in the street, on his back, looking up at the shining stars and naming the brightest ones after the women in his life who were *his own* shining stars.

But then the stars began to fade, as did everything else. And then everything went black for Vico.

CHAPTER 29

*F*our thuds against the front door woke Loreto from her sleep. As she looked around, she saw it was still dark. The night sky still sent a darkness over the city and over everything inside the house. She heard some voices whispering from the other room and then Uncle Charlie went stumbling by in his night clothes and down the stairs. She heard the door open and then some voices talking to Uncle Charlie.

Listening intently, she could hear some of the words coming from the speaker's mouth. The words were in English, which Uncle Charlie and Aunt Tomasina were learning to speak and teaching their children to do so as well, but Loreto, Lena, and Carolina were still working on getting accustomed to their new country.

Although she couldn't understand what they were

saying, she continued to listen. She was worried about her father. He hadn't come home from work that night, and she could barely sleep knowing he was still out in the city somewhere. The stress was obviously getting to him and she worried that he might have purposely not come home. That the sight of Uncle Charlie and Aunt Tomasina would only drive him deeper into a state of anxiety, knowing they were growing more and more impatient with him each day. The knock on the door worried her, and she thought maybe her father had done something to get himself arrested. So she listened intently, and as soon as she heard her father's name within the conversation, she jumped from the bed and went to the door.

Uncle Charlie was talking with two police officers. The policemen here looked similar to the few she had seen back in Italy, only these ones looked a little sadder. For some reason, when they looked at Loreto, they seemed to be even more so. She thought to herself that maybe they knew who she was and would be upset to tell her that her dad had landed himself in jail. That he wouldn't be coming home for the night—or maybe even for a while—and Loreto would once again be solely in charge of the girls.

The news Uncle Charlie would relay to her was something far worse. Something that took the breath from her lungs and sent her to her knees in a fit of agony. She screamed and it seemed to echo not only through the house, but out of the house and into the street, waking the neighbors who they had played alongside with for the last few weeks.

Loreto soon felt a warm, tight squeeze around her torso and then heard Aunt Tomasina in her ear, weeping along with her and trying to provide comfort. But there was no comfort. There was nothing but anguish and pain. Her father was dead. Gone. Forever. How could this have happened? They were so close to having the entire family back. So close to being Americans together like Vico had always desired.

As she and Aunt Tomasina sobbed, Uncle Charlie continued talking to the police. They spoke in English so she couldn't understand what they were saying, but she knew her uncle would tell her after. For now, she cried. And she cried even harder at the thought of Lena and Carolina making their way slowly, sleepily, and innocently toward the door when they heard all the noise. They would ask what was going on, and then their little hearts would be shattered when they heard the news. Their worlds would be broken, never again the same. Loreto wished she could figure out a way to protect them from having to endure the pain, but she knew deep down that she couldn't.

And then they came. All at once. Lena, Carolina, Maria, Carmella, Jimmy, Louise, and Anthony. All of them. Like a group of sleepwalkers pushing their way to the door. Just as they saw Loreto on the ground with her aunt's arms draped around her, Uncle Charlie shut the door and ended his conversation with the police. He turned, looked down at Loreto and then to the group of children standing before the three of them, waiting, wondering what they would hear. Uncle Charlie looked back down at Loreto and nodded to her, then lowered his head.

Loreto stood, releasing herself from Aunt Tomasina's grasp. She walked up to Lena and Carolina who stood with their cousins. She knelt down to get to Carolina's eye level and then she told them:

"Papà," she said. And then, through a new round of sobbing, said, "è morto." *He's dead*.

Lena screamed and Carolina looked up at her, wide-eyed, then back down at Loreto who was still on her knee. Loreto realized that she didn't fully understand what she had just been told and for that, Loreto was thankful. She didn't want to see either of her sisters have to cry and have to process the news. Lena was certainly in the immediate stages of grieving, but if Carolina could be spared it would help. After all, Loreto and Lena would certainly need some of her innocence to take their minds off of what was happening.

Questions started to come from the kids' mouths, and they were questions Loreto was preparing to ask once the initial shock had come to an end:

What happened?

How did they find him?

What happens now?

Loreto wanted to know everything. She wanted to know every word those policemen said to Uncle Charlie when they spoke in English. She wanted to know how her father died and who found him and who harmed him. And all the kids wanted to know as well, because they continued to ask.

Uncle Charlie sent his kids back to bed and motioned for Loreto to bring the girls to the kitchen table. He and Aunt Tomasina went there as well. And that's when they told them everything that happened. That patrons of Grotto Bar as well as some others living nearby heard the shots. Some ran outside to check on things and one of those people was a bartender at Grotto Bar. The police said her name was Julia Torolli and she stated to them that she thought she knew what happened and would be willing to talk to them.

"The policemen said they have detectives talking to her now," Uncle Charlie said.

Their aunt and uncle gave each of the girls a hug and then left them alone to weep and mourn in peace. After a while, the girls found themselves lying on the furniture where their dad should have been sleeping. Carolina wept for a bit, but seemed only to be doing so because her siblings were. Shortly after they made their way to the couch, she was asleep.

Not long after, Lena drifted off as well. Sitting up and uncomfortable, Loreto looked down at her two sisters whose heads rested snugly on each of her thighs. She had no idea what was in store for them next but knew that she would need to act like the responsible young woman she had to be on the boat and train that took them here. She would need to look after her sisters and figure out what they would do next.

Then the thought struck her: What *would* they do? Where would they go? Who would they live with? Mom was clearly too ill to make the long trip to America, and Uncle Charlie had begun to show visible signs of frustration that Dad hadn't made enough money to get the four of them into their own place yet. Either of those routes didn't seem to have a possible resolution in the short-term and that sent a wave of fear through Loreto. What would happen? Where would they end up?

She was only a sixteen-year-old girl, but she would now be the one who had to figure it all out. *In the morning, though*, she told herself. Then she leaned her head back on the chair, closed her eyes, and allowed herself to rest.

CHAPTER 30

The Cleveland Police had no problem solving her father's murder. With what the bartender, Julia Torolli, had said when she talked to them and the statement of other witnesses at the bar who saw the fight just an hour or so before the shooting, the suspect was easily found. And he admitted guilt when approached by the police officers.

For a brief moment, Loreto felt guilty. She felt like she let Mario walk all over her and the girls when they were on their trip, and if maybe she had been a little tougher on him, her father wouldn't have been so angry. But she let that thought quickly fade because she knew her father wouldn't have allowed her to think that way. Mario was a grown man who was paid to escort three young girls across the Atlantic Ocean and America's east coast. And he was paid handsomely, at that. If anything, *he* was the one who deserved the bullets and to be left dead in the middle of the street.

Within the house, her cousin Anthony was the best at writing so he was chosen to write a note home to their mother's friend, Gilda, to inform her of Vico's death. It saddened Loreto to think about her mother—a woman who was already suffering from such depression and brokenheartedness—to have to read this. She wondered how her mother would handle it.

In the days that followed Vico's death, Loreto and her sisters cried a bit more. Lena was old enough to wonder what would happen to them now, but still, Loreto had no clue. The only thing they knew so far was that Uncle Charlie was working with an undertaker to have their father's body prepared for a viewing at the house and that it wasn't cheap to do so. Although he was trying to keep a straight face in front of all the kids, he was having a tough time dealing with all of this financially.

On the afternoon when the viewing took place, friends from the neighborhood had come by to say their goodbyes to Vico. Loreto watched as men who had dirty fingernails and dressed in sweat-soaked clothes like her dad came through the door, and she could only guess they were from Asher Metalworks where Vico spent so many days. Then the neighbors came in to pay their respects, and two of the neighbors were Mr. and Mrs. Santangelo. They immediately went to Carolina to provide comfort, and although she did weep at the sight of her father in his state, she had quickly gotten over it and moved onto playing with her cousins again. Loreto envied that young innocence. The Santangelos offered to take her and keep an eye on her for a day or so, but Loreto kindly asked her aunt and uncle to decline. She wanted her sisters to remain together while they mourned—or at least as Lena and Loreto did.

Loreto received lots of condolences, and it made her feel good to know that her father had impacted the lives of so many. Even if they only met him once, they came to pay their respects and that made her happy.

The next morning, her father's body was laid to rest in the Catholic Cemetery on 128th Street, which was close enough for the girls to visit so long as they were still living with their aunt and uncle. And when the services were over and they said their final goodbye to their father, the girls went back to the house with their aunt, uncle, and cousins, and they grieved for the rest of the day. But in the morning, Loreto made sure she did something to help. She spent the day searching for a way to make money and found a job working inside of a wealthy home in Cleveland Heights. She was able to get to and from via a train car and no burden whatsoever would need to be placed on her aunt and uncle. She also made sure Lena was a help to Aunt Tomasina around the house and that Carolina was cleaning up after herself.

In a follow-up note she had asked Anthony to write to her mother, she informed her of her new occupation and how, with time, she would be able to buy a ticket for her mother to come to America. Loreto wrote in the letter that by the time she was healthy enough to travel, she would hopefully have enough money to fund the trip. She also made a promise to her mother that she would watch over Lena and Carolina in the meantime, and vowed not to let anything bad happen to them.

Loreto would also try to keep her aunt and uncle informed of her doings and what she was telling her mother back home. Although Carmina was still too sick to make the trip, Loreto tried to comfort her aunt and uncle by telling them that she would help as much as she could financially until their mother was able to come. Uncle Charlie was growing more and more stressed with his extra financial burden, but he was a kind man and she could see in his eyes that he was trying his best to help.

Finally, several weeks later, a letter came from Italy. To this point, Anthony had penned two letters to the home country and neither had been responded to. When this one came, Uncle Charlie wasn't home so it was Anthony who had to open it and read it to the girls.

Dearest Children, it began. *I am writing you with the heaviest of hearts as I must tell you my friend Carmina has passed away. On the 21ˢᵗ of this past month, her failing heart had finally given way.* The note went on to have a little more information in it about the farm and how it was being sold and that the girls would most likely inherit the sum—news that Uncle Charlie would be happy to hear—but all Loreto could wonder was what made her mother's heart finally fail for good. Was it the news of Vico? Had the letter even reached Carmina before she passed away? Did she even know what happened? Or was it the news of his death mixed with her depression and missing her girls that finally made her give up? Loreto thought it also might have been the depression of a life that could have been so much more. She had heard her mother tell stories every so often while Vico was in America about a young man named Antonio who she lost in a fishing boat accident when she was only sixteen. They were in love and to be together, but a storm had caused him to drown and never return home from a morning fishing trip.

The letter from Gilda went on to mention Vincenzo, Vico's brother, whom Gilda promised to reach out to with regard to the farm and its potential sale. She wrote that she would need to find him since it seemed no one had talked to him in several years, but that she would do her best to do so quickly.

When Uncle Charlie walked into the house that

evening, he was met by his wife with the letter and its contents. He was able to read it, and Loreto watched as his hand went over his mouth and his eyes widened. She could see in his face that he was more scared than upset. His first thought must have been the girls and what would happen with them. The financial struggles over the previous few weeks were a clear indicator that he couldn't continue to carry on like this, even if Loreto was chipping in with her new job.

He was nervous, but he was still a kind man and he spent time with each Carolina, Lena, and, finally, Loreto, telling them how sorry he was for what they'd had to go through recently. He promised that he and Tomasina would do anything to help, but when he said so to Loreto, there was a look in his eye that said he was already doing everything possible and he had no clue what more he could do.

The suggestion he would make was one that changed the course of history for the entire D'Imperio family.

CHAPTER 31

*L*oreto was doing all she could to try to bring money into the home and help out, but it was nearly impossible. Jobs for women were scarce and jobs for sixteen-year-old women were even more so. Uncle Charlie had said he would do everything possible to make sure the girls were safe, but it had been weeks since then and things weren't getting any better. Nor had Gilda written back regarding her search for Vincenzo to see if the land in Mirabella could be sold.

She would try to help in alternate ways, as well, like foregoing meals and having Carolina and Lena split their portions in order to preserve the food within the house. Lena would also clean and make sure that Carolina wasn't a burden while Loreto was working. But these were the only ways she could help. Just like Uncle Charlie struggled to come up with ways to support everyone financially, she struggled to find *any* additional way to chip in.

Each day, as she came home from work, she would glow with anticipation of another letter from Gilda arriving, but there were none. Days went by and then weeks, and soon three months had gone by and still nothing. Her hopes began to fade, and she ultimately became upset with the entire situation. She was ready to hit her breaking point. And as it turns out, she wasn't the only one.

Uncle Charlie asked Loreto after dinner one night to stay at the table with him. Once the children had cleaned the table, he retrieved some papers and sat down next to her. The papers were a list of his finances—how much money he brought in each week compared to how much he was spending. And the numbers, as he showed her, were leaning pretty heavily one way.

"I can't do it anymore," he told her in the only language she knew. "I'm sorry."

Loreto understood, but she couldn't comprehend what would happen. She asked him if there was anything else she could do but there was nothing. He said the money Loreto was making was enough for her to stay with them, but that Lena and Carolina would need other arrangements. For Lena, he suggested a new orphanage that was opening in a suburb east of Cleveland. And for Carolina, he had spoken with the Santangelos down the street who were thrilled at the idea of adopting her.

Her parents had always taught her the idea of respect. This is especially true with regard to your elders. And even more so with elders who have let you stay in their home for months. But the anger shot out of her and she stood from her chair and said, "You will *not* separate us!"

By this point, Aunt Tomasina had finished cleaning in the kitchen and joined them at the table. "We don't know what else we can do," she said.

And just as quickly as the anger shot out of her, so too did the statement that would be more than any sixteen-year-old would be willing to do in order to keep her siblings living together. "I will marry the first man who will have me as long as my sisters can remain living with me."

Her aunt and uncle looked at each other and then back at her. "The first man?" Aunt Tomasina asked. Then they both went on to ask her more questions about her future, about love, and about what she was about to sacrifice if she went through with this.

"I've lost my father and my mother and I'm not about to lose my sisters, too. I will do whatever it takes."

They both hugged her as if they might never see her again and Uncle Charlie, before walking away with his financial statements in-hand, said to her,

"Your sisters' lives have just been changed forever. They will thank you for it when they're older."

Over the next few days, word began to get around that this sixteen-year-old girl who was pretty and had a kind heart was seeking marriage. Although the options at the time were fewer than in recent years due to the war, he was still being approached about Loreto on a daily basis.

One of those who approached him was a 24-year-old named Gennaro Talamo.

CHAPTER 32

*L*oreto was nervous on the day she was set to meet a man her uncle had approved of.

His name was Gennaro and what she had learned about him through Uncle Charlie was that he grew up in a small town of Gildone, which was only a few miles from her hometown of Mirabella. She also learned that he was conflicted as to whether or not to go back to the old country to fight for Italy in the war, or to remain in America.

To go back and fight or not to go back and fight was a conflict for many young Italian men living in America. Gennaro, however, was fully prepared to stay if he would be awarded Loreto's hand in marriage.

Uncle Charlie had scheduled a meeting for the two of them at his house and when Gennaro arrived,

Loreto was called to the door. What she saw at first was a kind-looking man. His looks weren't bad, but they weren't anything that immediately struck her. However, once he smiled, his compassion and kindness showed through.

"Ciao. È un piacere conoscerti," he said to her. *Hi. It's nice to meet you.* And when he said it, he said so softly.

They spoke for a bit inside the house and Gennaro told her that he had seen her around—playing in the street with her sisters or catching the train car to go to work—and he found her to be very beautiful. He continued to flatter her, and that's when she reminded him that a marriage to her meant her sisters would be able to live with them as well.

To her surprise, and relief, he said he would love that, and then asked if he could meet them. The girls came downstairs and met Gennaro and it was all smiles. Loreto introduced her sisters to him and then she stood back and watched how he would interact with them. And he treated them both perfectly. He treated Lena as a blossoming young girl and Carolina as an energetic child.

At that very moment, she knew her future. This man who she had never met before was going to be her husband. She would forfeit the chance at finding random love on the train car, at church, or around in the city. She would marry this man, bear his children, keep his home, and grow old with him, all so that her sisters would remain with her. And while the thoughts of what she was sacrificing were sad for sure, there would be nothing sadder than watching her sisters be split up and, over time, grow apart.

In the Fall of 1918, Loreto married Gennaro and the four of them—Gennaro, Loreto, Lena, and Carolina—moved into a two-bedroom apartment on 132nd Street. It was close enough to where they could visit Uncle Charlie, Aunt Tomasina, and the kids, and it was nice to be able to visit and see that they were able to get back to normal life. The four chairs that Vico had to buy when they moved in were no longer around the kitchen table, and there was a smile on Uncle Charlie's face that didn't seem to be there for the last few weeks they were living with him.

Loreto and Gennaro started their family and eventually had four children of their own. Lena and Carolina would remain under the same roof until they themselves were married and living in their own home. They helped Loreto with the children so much that Lena and Carolina were considered by the four to be their sisters.

There were certainly struggles that came along with an arranged marriage, and Loreto knew that going into it. But when those issues arose, she took them in stride. She handled issues with her husband lovingly and tenderly because she remembered that he was the reason she and her sisters were able to remain together. And she and Gennaro stayed married all the way up until her passing in 1978.

Lena would go on to marry and have a child of her own and Carolina would do the same and have two children. They remained close for their entire lives, and they made sure their children remained close as well. In fact, they remained so close that they lived next door to each other for many years. They would also enjoy the company of the paesani who continued to come to America from Campobasso and the life they would all live peacefully in the new country.

The story of these three sisters would be told around many dinner tables and gatherings. It was a tale of true love and sacrifice. A tale of a sixteen-year-old girl giving up her life in order to keep her nine- and three-year-old sisters with her. It was a story that was gut-wrenching and heartwarming at the same time, and Loreto would always be revered for what she did to keep her family together.

Lena would be remembered, too, because she was always considered to be the rock of the family—always there when needed.

Carolina, although very young when all of this happened and unable to contribute as much as the others, was still a big part growing up within the family of Gennaro and Loreto. She was closest to Loreto's children's ages and grew close to them. While Lena took more of a motherly approach to helping Loreto, Carolina played the part of friend to the children. And she, too, would go on to marry and start her own family. Carolina would have two sons and several grandchildren.

And of those two sons, I'd like to think I was her favorite. For you see, she was my mother.

(From left to right): Lena, Loreto, and Carolina

The only remaining picture of The Sisters from Campobasso as children.

EPILOGUE

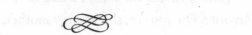

 *resent Day.*

As Mike waited in the airport terminal to board the plane back to Phoenix, he looked out the tall windows exposing the planes parked at their gates. Rain poured down from a cloudy sky that matched his somber mood. He was leaving Cleveland, going back to the place he now called home. He was widening his family roots, and it made him feel guilty doing so. Everyone else remained in the city where Grandpa Vico first came to live with his Uncle Charlie, and Mike was the first to leave.

As information about his flight's boarding was being called overhead, he thought about the time he was able to spend in the city where he was raised. Saying goodbye to his cousin Laura saddened him and made him realize just how fragile life was. It seemed like just yesterday when he, Laura, and the other cousins would play in the streets and go to each other's houses for dinners and holidays. Now, they were all parents and grandparents of their own. Time had certainly flown by.

Mike walked down the jetway and onto the plane where he was greeted by a smiling airline crew. They had no idea what he had just been through—were clueless as to how his family tree in America was on the brink of being deteriorated and information lost in the process. Mike was simply a customer to them, so they greeted him with a smile. And as they did, he wondered about *their* families. About *their* family trees and *their* roots.

He took his window seat and looked out into the damp and cloudy sky. Droplets of rain hit the window. There was commotion as fellow passengers took their seats and searched for overhead storage room for their bags. When he focused a bit more, he recognized that nobody else seemed to be in a situation like his. Nobody else seemed concerned about how quickly life was passing by and whether or not important family members would be forgotten.

His eyes welled with tears when the plane lifted off from Cleveland's Hopkins International Airport.

And as the world beneath him got smaller and smaller and the flight attendants and pilots made continual messages throughout the cabin, those feelings amplified. At Laura's funeral, he saw so many people that he, Laura, and the other cousins would play with as kids. He saw distant relatives, old neighbors, and friends who were once close enough to be considered family. And what he realized was that he missed them. He missed his life in Cleveland. He missed his family and although he moved to Arizona for the peace, a part of him wanted the chaos back. Mike wanted to see his family. To be able to share the story of the sisters of Campobasso with them and to make sure their story was always remembered. After saying goodbye to Laura and realizing how quickly the elder family members could begin to fade away, he wanted to ensure Aunt Loreto's courage was known for generations to come.

The story of his mother and her sisters was never one he took lightly. Mike knew of the struggles and marveled in how far their family had come since the days of Grandpa Vico working in the foundry. He felt blessed to be able to get onto a plane and move to another state without so much as a shrug of his shoulders and a thought of *Why not?* As he looked down onto the grassy farmlands of Illinois and Indiana, he quietly thanked his mother, Carolina. He thanked Aunt Loreto and Aunt Lena for their bravery and what they had done, unknowingly, for future generations of their family. And then he did what he always did when he thought about the bravery of his mother and her sisters: he prayed. Mike lowered his head and began, "Hail Mary..."

ABOUT THE AUTHOR

Don Dimberio is an 83-year-old first time author. After graduating from the University of Notre Dame, he spent most of his career in the plastics industry.

Since he was a young man, the true life story of his mother and her sisters begged to be told. As he recounted their story over the years, he was encouraged to share this incredible story of the courage and love of a woman for her sisters.

His words pertaining to this story are what led him to write this book:

"My mother and her sisters had to go through what no young children should have to go through. I'm proud of what they were able to accomplish. This story is not only a tribute to these three ladies, but to all the undervalued stories of hardship. So many stories get lost through the generations and I'd like this story to be one that begins the trend of generational stories carrying on over time."